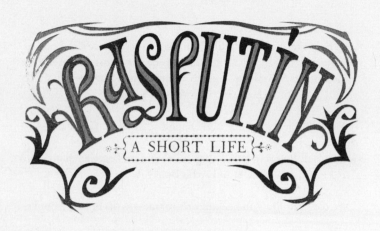

RASPUTIN
A SHORT LIFE

FRANCES WELCH

MARBLE ARCH
PRESS

To my brother Nick

YAKUTSK•

IRKUTSK•

CHINA

JAPAN

Map of Russia in the early 1900s

The wisest men follow their own directions
And listen to no prophet guiding them.
None but the fools believe in oracles,
Forsaking their own judgement. Those who know,
Know that such men can only come to grief.

Euripides – *Iphigenia In Tauris*

'I Feel My End Is Near'

On Grigory Rasputin's last day alive the snow fell heavily upon St Petersburg. The sky at dawn had been dotted with what the Tsarina called picturesquely 'wee pink clouds'. But the weather had then closed in, with severe frosts sending temperatures plummeting below freezing.

Rasputin's daughter Maria claimed that no living Russian could remember a harsher winter than that of 1916. The 18-year-old Maria found herself confined to her father's flat, where the fusty rooms steamed with fetid warmth and the pervasive smell was of cabbage and hot sheep's cheese.

The streets outside usually pullulated with her father's followers, the so-called 'Rasputinki'. Up to 400 had been known to gather before sunrise, waiting as long as three days to see him.

Grigory Rasputin's name was by this time known the length and breadth of Russia: he was the Siberian peasant 'Holy Man' who had inveigled his way into the heart of the splendid pre-Revolutionary Court. His mysterious rise had made him an object of hatred, fear and reverence.

His claims as a Holy Man, ridiculed and dismissed by some, were accepted, without question, by many who believed he had been sent by God. Devotees came in search of curious keepsakes: burnt rusks in scented hankies or soiled linen, limp with sweat. The most fervent took Rasputin's fingernail clippings, to be sewn into hemlines, despite one St Petersburg restaurant manager testifying that the Man of God's hands were 'grimy, with bitten, blackened nails'.

It was known that Grigory Rasputin had the ears of 'the Tsars', as he called the Tsar and Tsarina. He also had a reputation for being free with rudimentary petitions along the lines of 'fix it, G'. So, alongside the devotees would be favour-seekers, filing through the lobby and up to the third floor, bearing lavish gifts: wine, carpets and even huge fish. Flowers were a favourite: 'Idiots bring fresh flowers every day. They know I love them,' Rasputin would swagger ungraciously.

Some of the 'Rasputinki' arrived with wads of money, others were penniless and in need. Unable to count, Rasputin would bark: 'Come on, fork it over,' before grabbing wads and redistributing them at random. One widow, who had lost sons in the war, was awarded 23,000 roubles. But most were not so lucky, despite Rasputin's regular, grand address to the queue: 'I will help you all!'

On December 16, however, Maria Rasputin peered out of the window and noted that Gorokhovaya Street was empty.

In fact, there had been odd bursts of activity through the day, beginning with the drunken return of her father in the early hours. Rasputin was an uninhibited drinker and, within the preceding few days, had pulled off a restaurant's door bell and smashed a pane of glass in the door of his flat. His police security guards described him on such raucous returns variously as: 'very drunk', 'completely drunk', 'dead drunk' and 'overcome with drink'. Maria had challenged her father about his drinking, but he was unabashed: 'Why shouldn't I drink? I am a man, like the others.' He considered wine 'God's own remedy.'

The Tsarina Alexandra, ever supportive of the man she referred to fondly either as 'our Friend' or 'Gr', made only one reference to Rasputin's weakness, once describing him as 'very gay after dinner in the vestry, but not tipsy'.

Shortly after this particular return, the Man of God, known for his fakir-like shunning of sleep, was back on the street. A brief lie-down had set him up for his next trip, to his beloved 'banya', the bath-house, where he would have his genitals soaped by one of the 'little ladies', as he called his women followers. Before succumbing to the soaping he would shout, confusingly: 'Demons of lechery, get thee hence!' When his daughter remonstrated with him about women, he was equally unabashed. 'If Christ could speak with Mary Magdalene...', he would say, or, more graphically: 'It doesn't matter if you fornicate a little.'

These rousing sessions at the bath-house would be followed by brisk walks to the nearest church, during

Above: Grigory Rasputin
Below: At tea with the Tsarina and two of the Grand Duchesses

which he slapped his upper arms and rebuked Satan. At church, he would enjoy a well-earned prayer. As he said repeatedly: 'Without sin there is no repentance.'

In recent weeks Rasputin's movements had been more erratic than usual. He had grown wary of leaving Number 64. His privileged position at Court had made him enemies, and his innate, primitive paranoia had been fuelled by real threats. Within the last two and a half years at least ten attempts had been made on his life; he had been targeted and nearly hit by sledges, set upon by officers with sabres and stabbed, almost fatally, by a woman. In another incident, during the summer of 1915, a second woman had been leaving the flat when Rasputin had identified her, too, as a would-be assassin. Upon his command – 'Drop what you have in your muff!' – a gun had clattered to the floor.

A month earlier, filled with morbid dread, he had written to his wife in Siberia, bidding farewell to his family. On parting from his son at the beginning of November, he had pronounced: 'Goodbye, I will never see you again'. He had informed Maria gloomily: 'I see a sort of black cloud over our St Petersburg house' and written her a letter, with the instruction: 'Don't open it until I'm dead.' When Tsar Nicholas had asked for a blessing at their last meeting, a fortnight before, Rasputin had replied: 'It is you who should be blessing me.'

However, two days previously, on December 14, Rasputin had successfully ventured out to two of St Petersburg's grandest cathedrals. The Tsarina, whom he had seen four days earlier, described the outing ecstatically to her husband. As a granddaughter of Queen

Victoria, she had grown up speaking English and the Imperial couple communicated in English. But her writing style remained idiosyncratic: 'Our Friend never goes out since ages, except to come here, but yesterday he walked in the streets with Munia [Maria Golovin, one of his most faithful and distinguished supporters] to the Kazan and St Isaacs & not one disagreeable look, people all quiet.'

On this last morning, the devoted Munia was with him again. She had braved blizzards to bring messages, including news of a successful petition: the dropping of a charge against Rasputin's secretary. The Tsarina had written peremptorily to her husband: 'I beg you to write "discontinue the case" & send it to the Minister of Justice... Otherwise... there can be disagreeable talks.'

Over a full ten hours (midday to 10.00pm) Munia carried out chores for the man she called Father Grigory. In his egalitarian household, princesses and countesses might be found peeling potatoes and dishing out jellied fish, while servants relaxed at table. Munia, whose mother had been a maid to two empresses, helped other followers with their overshoes.

According to Munia, Rasputin seemed happier than he had been for a while, but still enigmatic: 'He was excited and said "Today I'm going", though he wouldn't say where.' His good spirits remained, even after another visitor, an elderly woman, had quizzed him about the future of Russia and he had issued one of his gloomy but curiously accurate prophecies: 'Little mother, I feel my end is near. They'll kill me, and then the throne won't last three months.' Such confidences would have been unusual; he preferred to keep older women at bay, snapping: 'Get away, you old carcass!' or 'I have no use for old goats!'

The freezing weather may have reduced the number of visitors. It did nothing to silence the telephone, which rang throughout the day. He had been woken that morning by a call from the Tsarina's closest friend, Anna Vyrubova. Rasputin received such routine calls from Anna or the Tsarina, or both, on a daily basis. There was nothing unusual about this last one.

According to the son of one of the Tsar's doctors, telephone calls from the Tsarina would be heralded by the 'lugubrious voice' of a male operator: 'You are called from the apartments of Her Imperial Majesty.' With no specific name mentioned, the receiver of the call would be obliged, unsettlingly, to guess who was on the line. The main telephone at the Alexander Palace was in the Tsarina's mauve boudoir, wired up under a portrait of Marie Antoinette.

Rasputin had become an unexpected fan of the telephone. He would jump to, answering it himself and greeting the caller in a raspy voice, with a rich Siberian accent: 'Here is Grishka.' In the peasant tradition, he usually referred to himself in the third person. He performed stark telephone cures. Once, when told that the sickly Tsarevich Alexis had an earache, he called the boy to the line: 'Your ear doesn't hurt. Grishka is telling you... Sleep right now.' Fifteen minutes later the Palace rang to say the Tsarevich had fallen asleep.

In the last few weeks, however, the telephone had become a menace. His surprisingly long number –

646-46 – was widely known and he had begun to receive calls cursing him. His responses were of the 'eye for an eye' variety. One caller said: 'Your days are numbered,' to which he snapped back: 'As for you, you will shortly die like a dog.' The day before his death, he received a call from a woman: 'Can you tell me where the funeral service for Rasputin will take place?' He replied: 'You'll be buried first!' On his last morning he was thrown, though only momentarily, by yet another anonymous call threatening his life.

During a brief lull in the snowfall that afternoon, he received a visit from the Tsarina's friend, Anna Vyrubova. She had come to ask his opinion about a pain in Alexis's leg. His reply was sanguine: 'It is not serious. Just keep the doctors away from him and he will be all right.' He offered a further, less accurate, prediction: 'Grishka can tell you this much. Throughout the rest of his life Alexis will not be seriously ill again.'

Anna Vyrubova had brought an icon as a gift from the Tsarina. It was signed by the Tsar and Tsarina and their five children and came from the city of Novgorod where, a few days before, the Tsarina had visited an ancient prophetess. The prophetess, in mortifying chains despite her 107 years, had addressed the Tsarina flatteringly: 'And you, the beautiful one, do not fear the heavy cross.' In fact, the formidable Tsarina had aged beyond her 44 years. Her facial expression was a daunting mix of hauteur and pain: the legacy of an already troubled life.

The icon from Nizhny Novgorod would form the last tangible bond between the Tsarina and her precious

'Gr'. The Tsarina regarded their relationship as a sort of partnership, at one point closing her instructions to the Tsar with a robust 'Listen to your staunch wifey and our Friend.'

Anna Vyrubova now commented on Rasputin's appearance: 'What about you, Grishka? You do not seem to be in very good health.' That was probably an understatement. He was showing the effects of a late-night session more or less running into a long lunch. One friend testified that, in the course of that day, Rasputin had drunk 12 bottles of his favourite Madeira before passing out.

Though aged just 47, Rasputin's appearance was not good: his close-set eyes were ringed with yellow excrescences. The irises, said to be so dazzling that their colour couldn't be determined – grey, blue and even blue and brown – were dulled. His broad nose was pock-marked, his lips blue and his moustaches protruding like worn-out brushes. Following years of use as a napkin, his straggling beard was festooned with decaying food.

His poor personal hygiene had not helped. The French Ambassador in St Petersburg, Maurice Paleologue, said he 'carried with him a strong animal smell, like the smell of a goat'. The singer Bellin talked of his rotten teeth and foul breath. His friend Aron Simanovich, the jeweller to the Imperial family, admitted that Rasputin had 'teeth like blackened stumps'.

Rasputin batted off Anna's concern, growling: 'I am like a horse, nothing affects me.' But his maid, Katya, weighed in: 'He should get more sleep.' Rasputin retorted that he was not planning an early night: he had an assignation with one of the richest aristocrats in Russia, Prince Felix Yussoupov, who was to pick him up at midnight and take him to his palace. There he would be introduced to Yussoupov's wife, the Tsar's beautiful young niece, Princess Irina.

Anna Vyrubova later testified at a commission conducted by the Provisional Government in 1917: 'I knew that Felix had often visited Rasputin, but it struck me as odd that he [Rasputin] should go to their house, for the first time, at such an unseemly hour.' She urged him not to go. But she was less concerned about his security than his status: he should not go to the Yussoupovs' Moika Palace unless he was being invited openly, at a normal time.

As Anna Vyrubova left the flat, she hesitated and Rasputin uttered what would be his last words to her: 'What more can you ask of me? You already have all I have to give.' Later that afternoon, Anna Vyrubova visited the Tsarina and mentioned Rasputin's plan. The Tsarina was bemused, as she knew that Princess Irina was, at that point, not in St Petersburg but far away in the Crimea.

According to his daughter Maria, Rasputin's last supper at the apartment was an unexpectedly jolly affair, during which he joked and played with her, her younger sister Varya, aged 16, and his young niece, Anna. He plunged his fingers readily into his fish and black bread and honey. After supper, he cheerily showed Maria a stash of 3,000 roubles, stored in a drawer for her dowry. He read his daughters the opening of the Gospel of St

John: 'In the beginning was the word...' Maria wrote: 'For the first time I could feel the beauty and truth of those mystic passages.'

But running alongside Maria's reverential memory is the less wholesome testimony of the hall porter, who noted a further visit that evening: 'A lady of about 25 was with him from 10.00 to 11.00pm'. This lady was also spotted by Rasputin's niece Anna, who clearly had few illusions about her uncle. She recalled that 'around 10pm a plump, blonde woman arrived called "Sister Maria", though she was no sister of mercy. She helped him to remove the tension that apparently took hold of him against his will.' Rasputin and 'Sister Maria' immediately retired to a little room where they set about removing that tension.

At some point that evening, Maria had taken herself out into the blizzard. She returned at 11pm, missing 'Sister Maria', but in time to catch the next visitor, Alexander Protopopov, the Minister of the Interior. Protopopov was himself a controversial character, in the advanced stages of syphilis and rumoured to be a necrophiliac. He regularly visited the flat, mostly at the behest of the Tsarina, who hoped the curious pair would discuss the country's troubles and that 'our Friend' might offer helpful tips.

Protopopov allegedly told Rasputin's daughters to leave the room so that he could talk to their father in private. Testifying later, however, he made no mention of the girls: 'I stopped by to see Rasputin... around 12.00. I... saw him for about ten minutes and saw only him since he opened the door himself. He didn't say anything to me about intending to go out.' If he had, Protopopov insisted he would have remonstrated with him: the Tsarina had specifically told him not to let our Friend leave his flat. He made a point, nevertheless, of warning Rasputin that he had heard of a plot against his life.

Rasputin did mention his plans to his daughter, Maria. As she testified: 'After I got back and was going off to bed, Father told me that he was going to visit "The Little One"'. Rasputin's nickname for Yussoupov was, confusingly, the same as the one used by the Tsarina for her son, Alexis. He also told his niece where he was going. But Maria added that none of them would have been in the least surprised, as the strikingly handsome and charming young Prince, then aged 29, had become 'for us, my sister and myself, the friend of the household'.

Rasputin also phoned his friend Simanovich, that night, to tell him that he was seeing Yussoupov. Simanovich's loyalty had been assured after Rasputin cured his son of the shaking disease, St Vitus' Dance. Simanovich himself, it seemed, had heard of a murder plot, and was sufficiently worried to warn his friend not to go out, then to insist he call again at 2am. That call never came.

Who the last visitor to the flat was that night was to become a matter of dispute. After dismissing Protopopov, Rasputin changed his clothes for the third time that day. Owing either to excitement or drink, he was unable to dress himself, and Katya had to help him into his favourite light-blue shirt, embroidered with cornflowers: 'He couldn't button the collar and I buttoned it for him.'

He wore a golden sash and his best pair of blue panta-loons; he also put on a bracelet with a monogram of the Tsar. Then he retired to his bedroom. As his niece Anna testified: 'Uncle lay down on his bed just after 12 in his clothing.'

Katya felt uneasy and lay awake. She slept in the kitchen, in a bed sealed off by a curtain. She later said that 'the bell rang at the back door'. After a few minutes, she heard voices, peeked through her curtain and rec-ognised Prince Felix Yussoupov.

But, in an early police interrogation, Yussoupov denied having been to the flat: 'Around 12.30 Raspu-tin called me from somewhere... inviting us to go to the gypsies... voices could be heard over the phone as well as a woman's squeal.' The idea of the Tsarina's Man of God telephoning from a noisy venue, in the style of a breathless teenager, apparently did not give rise to com-ment. But then the police would have been too over-awed by Yussoupov's connections to question him fur-ther. It would have been unthinkable to take the word of Rasputin's peasant maid, Katya, over that of the Tsar's nephew.

Whether Yussoupov intended to carry on lying can-not be known. But, with his strong sense of theatre, he was soon finding the colourful truth too hard to con-tain. Within days, he was revelling in the telling of a wholly different sequence of events, beginning with his first glimpse of Rasputin at the flat door. He noted the efforts of the Man of God to clean himself up: Rasputin had combed the food out of his beard and now smelt of cheap soap. Later reports said that he had also covered his ears and neck with cologne. He took an unexpected pride in his ability to brush up, occasionally calling for scissors for his fingernails and perfumed pomatum for his stringy hair. Maria wrote, however, that, despite all his pains, her father had begun to feel apprehensive about the arrangement. She reported that he said to Yussoupov: 'Must I leave tonight?'

Maria herself was nervous. Though they were not suspicious of Yussoupov, Maria and her sister Varya had become worried about their father leaving the flat after dark. As he struggled to find his boots, he said: 'It's those children again, they have hidden them. They don't want me to go out.' But he finally found the boots and was ready to go. Maria, who, like Katya, had been unable to sleep, made unsuccessful attempts to comfort herself with her father's maxim: 'Nothing can happen to me unless it's God's will.'

In her testimony to the police on December 18 Maria Rasputin said: 'Later I went to sleep and did not see whether "The Little One" arrived and whether he and my father left together.'

Years later, however, the fanciful Maria told a different story. She described herself back at her window, watching her father walking along the street, pulling up his collar and making the sign of the cross. She wrote that she wept as she watched him getting into a car with Yussoupov; and swore that, as the motor fired up, she spotted an elegant hand reach out to shut the car door.

Rasputin never had any difficulty reconciling his weakness for beautiful young princesses with a passion for the simple life. During his last years, he spent many a happy hour at palaces repeating one of his favourite instructions: 'Be glad at simplicity.' He was full of invitations as unlikely as they were picturesque: 'Come with me in the summer... to the open spaces of Siberia. We will catch fish and work in the fields. And then you will really learn to understand God.'

He evidently wanted his listeners to know he set great store by his Siberian origins. But, as with so many of Rasputin's pronouncements, it is hard to gauge the extent of his sincerity.

What is certain is that the spiritual pride of puritans was among his biggest bugbears. The traditional Siberian had no qualms about embracing wine, women and song. In this Wild East of Russia, if a man could prove he had been drunk when attacking a judge, he would get only three days in prison. A Siberian picnic comprised a parcel of fresh cucumbers and a hearty pail of wine. According to one contemporary traveller, female binge drinkers in comic headgear lined the streets on freezing winter nights. The traveller described one incident during which the women hurled snow at men, then, in a grand crescendo, fell down and threw up their legs, 'revealing the most remarkable sights'.

The prevailing hedonism was combined with mystical fervour. Hunters in Siberia were reputedly able to teleport themselves from covey to covey. Religious sects flourished in the forests, ranging from groups of Old Believers quibbling over alterations in the liturgy to fanatics burning themselves to death. In extreme sects, baptisms by fire included male castration; women had their nipples and clitorises cut off while holding icons.

Pilgrims, '*stranniki*', wandered through the villages, telling spell-binding stories of their travels in return for food and a bed. Villagers left bowls of food and milk on their doorsteps; these would be snapped up by the *stranniki*, vagrants or escaped convicts, whoever was first. In Pokrovskoye, where Rasputin grew up, the bowls would have been particularly appreciated by the pigs that wandered freely up and down its main street.

In Rasputin's day, the village comprised 1,000 people in 200 houses. The villagers endured harsh winters, with temperatures dropping to minus 50, followed by spring thaws which reduced the rough main track to a sea of liquid mud.

The Rasputins were one of Pokrovskoye's oldest established families, with roots dating back to 1643. Rasputin's supporters have been quick to point out that the family name was derived from '*rasput*', meaning 'crossroad', and not '*rasputnik*', debauchee, as was sometimes claimed. Indeed, in the early 1800s, Rasputin's forebears, Ivan and Miron Rosputin (sic), were listed among the village's 'better souls'.

Whether Rasputin's father, Efim, carried on in the 'better souls' family tradition is a matter of argument. According to some reports, he liked strong vodka and was a 'deplorable drunkard'. Though primarily heterosexual, he successfully cultivated young male lovers: this despite his appearance: 'chunky, unkempt and stooped'.

But at his funeral the family spoke of his religious

dedication and untiring work on the farm. His dutiful granddaughter, Maria, portrayed him as a gentleman of the old school, sipping China tea while railing against the horse thieves who blighted the 'better souls" lives: canny thieves would lasso their prey then make silent escapes, with the horses' hooves wrapped in rags.

It was claimed, by his supporters, that Efim Rasputin acquired conversational skills and wisdom through his job driving carts. This seems unlikely. He certainly took pride in his work, flaunting a smart carter's badge on his left arm and a cap with an Imperial eagle. But rides on his route, 'Trakt 4', linking Tyumen and Tobolsk, were so rough that passengers in the clattering carts were obliged to lie full length on piles of hay to save their spines.

Maria's claim that Efim read the Bible to his family also seems far-fetched. In an 1877 census, conducted when little Grishka was eight, Efim indicated, with crosses, that the whole family was illiterate. Twenty-two years later, another census revealed that no progress had been made: the Rasputins, now including Grigory's wife Praskovia, were still unable to read or write.

Rasputin's mother, Anna, was described in one report as 'short and rotund' but in another as 'tall, slim with shining eyes'. The photographic evidence is flawed, as the images are blurred and there are conflicting captions. One indistinct photograph of her apparently exists in which she peers intently at the camera, perhaps suspicious of the new technology. Her loyal granddaughter, Maria, claimed that Anna kept a meticulously clean house.

Rasputin's parents married in 1862, when Efim was 20 and Anna 22. The Rasputins were relatively well off, apparently occupying an *izba* with an unlikely sounding eight rooms and owning 12 cows and 18 horses. They may have used their yard as a latrine, but they were not reduced to creating windows out of stretched animal bladders.

The miasma of confusion surrounding Rasputin's life begins in his childhood. Rumours and counter-rumours have sprung up, even concerning several mysterious siblings.

Much has been made of real evidence that his parents lost four children before Rasputin was born; it has been suggested that this was some kind of divine warning. Three sons born after him also died. There may have been one surviving sister, Feodosia. Some biographies mention a brother, Misha or Dmitri, and a sister, Vara, who helped in the house; allusions have been made to a second epileptic sister, who fell into the river and drowned while doing the laundry.

Amid these confusing details, it is perhaps understandable that, in her memoir, Maria got her own father's birth date – January 9 1869 – wrong. Rasputin himself misled people, sometimes adding as much as eight years to his age. Considering himself a sort of elder to the Imperial family, he disliked being younger than the Tsar, who was born a year before him.

According to Maria, her father's birth was marked with a comet across the sky. Others claimed that babies were born that day with iron teeth and dogs with six legs; it was said that snakes fell from the sky.

The stark contradictions that were to mark Rasputin's life began shortly after his birth. Though his birth weight was an average seven pounds, he was freakishly advanced physically: standing at six months and walking at eight. This physical prowess was not matched, however, by any mental development and he was unable to speak until he was two and a half. His mother, Anna, became increasingly worried as the toddler stared interminably at the sky and at individual blades of grass. She thought he 'was not quite right in the head'. She might have been relieved if she had advance knowledge of the 1917 Commission's conclusion that there was no history of mental illness in the Rasputin family.

His propensity for being virtually catatonic alternated with periods of great restlessness. When he was not holed up in the *izba*, staring fearfully at shadows, he would be running amok in the forest. He wet his bed, and cried so frequently that he was known as 'sniveller' and 'snot nose'. Aged eight, he was swimming in a river with his cousin Dmitri when the boys got into difficulties. Though they were both rescued, Dmitri died of pneumonia shortly afterwards. In his grief, the young Grishka went off his food, barely touching his favourite pickled fish and stuffed eggs.

Rasputin was 12 when his mystical gifts became apparent. First it was discovered that the family cows produced more milk if he was nearby. Then he cured a lame horse by placing his hand on its hamstring and throwing his head back. He was soon able to predict when a stranger was on the way; an hour after his announcement, a traveller would appear, in the distance, on Trakt 4.

On one occasion, when he was lying ill, the boy overheard his father and friends discussing a recent horse theft. He struggled off his sick bed, came into the kitchen and pointed to the richest peasant: 'He's the one who stole the horse.' The villagers followed the man home, discovered the stolen horse and, Siberian-style, beat the man half to death. Grishka claimed he never stole as a boy because he had visions of thieves ringed by their ill-gotten gains.

As a child, Rasputin was not up for the usual Siberian games of convicts and soldiers. Nor did he attend school; in this he inadvertently followed the teaching of his namesake, Saint Grigory, who viewed learning as one of life's obstacles. He eventually grew to enjoy some regular boyish pursuits: gorging on salted cucumbers, hunting, fishing and dancing the Kazachok, with bent knee. But he remained isolated, spending particularly desolate hours sitting by the roadside, thrashing himself with thistles. As he admitted: 'I was an outsider.'

His physical strength ensured that, despite his isolation, he was never a victim of bullying. Indeed, he succeeded in beating up the village bully, Boris, to some extent even stealing his crown. He was clearly impulsive. He once assaulted a beggar woman but, because of his age, there was no inquiry. He threw a 15-month-old girl into the river because she wouldn't smile at him. At 14 he nearly killed a man who tried to rob him, for which he was punished with 20 strokes of the whip. A doctor who treated him for smallpox was impressed by the 'ardent expression' in his eyes but also described him as the 'terror of the district'.

Perhaps it was lucky that his violent impulses were tempered by a taste for mysticism. The desperate village priest offered the young terror bribes to stay away from Sunday services. But ten kopecks was not enough to keep Grishka from the white church with gilded domes that dominated Pokrovskoye. He even claimed to enjoy discussions about the scriptures with his one friend, called, like his dead cousin, Dmitri. As he said of his adolescence: 'I dreamt of God many times... I wept without knowing why or where my tears came from.'

He was so thrilled when he first heard about the 'Kingdom of God within you' that he had a vision of a bright light. The vision came to him while he was sitting under a larch tree. Years later, when Maria was aged ten, he took her to the same larch tree and told her how he had realised, then, that 'God is here, inside, this moment – for ever.' When he told his timorous mother that he'd 'almost seen God', she was worried that he had blasphemed and told him not to mention the vision to his excitable father.

Rasputin's enjoyment of the female form began innocently enough, watching fellow villagers skinny-dipping. At 16, however, he underwent some sort of sexual assault by the young wife of a general. Maria's description of the assault leaves little to the imagination. Her information concerning the seamier side of her father's life came from another of Rasputin's maids, Dounia, aunt of the maid Katya. Dounia never shrank from telling Maria the fruitier details. The young girl kept a meticulous record of their chats in a school notebook.

Maria describes how Rasputin was enticed by the general's wife to a summer house on her large estate. She reached down his trousers, 'grasped him gently, releasing him for a moment then touching him again'. After the grasps, she lay on a bed, gazing at him provocatively. Apparently he was about to pounce, when four maidservants appeared from behind curtains. These maidservants humiliated him, throwing water over him and 'touching his out-thrust organ'.

Fortunately for the young Grishka, Dounia was one of the maidservants. Seeing him for the first time, aged 14, she was immediately smitten. She took pity on him, found his scattered clothes and returned them to him. Dounia may have been captivated by his out-thrust organ; she was unlikely to have been attracted by his face. As a result of innumerable scraps, his large nose was already slightly askew and looked, according to one account, as if it had been slapped on with a trowel.

This first sexual experience marked Rasputin's debut as a serial seducer of women. From now on he would feel free to accost young women of all shapes and sizes, kissing them while struggling with vital buttons.

But for all these insensitive fumblings, the teenage Grishka sometimes showed a soft heart. Later that same year, he saw a naked widow being dragged through the streets by a horse. She was being punished, according to the local custom, after having been found sleeping with a vagabond. Grishka pursued her into the forest and built her a hideaway. He visited her several times but, in a surprising turn-up for the books, left what remained of her honour intact: his restraint here is particularly laudable as she was purportedly the first woman he healed with caresses to the buttocks.

It was during a visit to a religious fete in a monastery at Avalak, on the River Tobol, in 1886, that Grishka met his future wife, Praskovia Dubrovina. When they parted, Maria reported that her father left a 'fervent kiss upon her willing lips'. It has been claimed that Praskovia, then aged 20, already felt left on the shelf and that her subsequent forbearance towards Grigory, then 17, stemmed from relief at being rescued from spinsterhood. But she seems to have had all the right attributes: she was plump, with dark eyes, small features and thick blonde hair. Though short, she was strong, an important asset in a wife expected to bear children while tackling the harvest. Photographs exist of the burly young Grishka but Praskovia is always absent.

Grishka and Praskovia were married five months later, on February 2 1887, three weeks after the groom's 18th birthday. Their first child was born the following year, but died at six months of scarlet fever. There was then a mysteriously long gap before the couple had twins, who both died of whooping cough. Could the rampant Grishka have restrained himself a full six years? That seems unlikely. But it seems almost more unlikely that the obliging Praskovia was keeping him at bay. In any case, they finally had their three surviving children: Dmitri in 1895, Maria in 1898 and Varya in 1900. A seventh child also died.

Rasputin proved a trying husband. His defenders claim it was his mother Anna's early death that drove him to drink. But then, according to some reports, Anna did not die until 1904.

Either way, it was during his early years of marriage that he got into the habit of driving carts to Tyumen to collect grain, then returning on foot, penniless and drunk. He sold the family bread to get money for alcohol. At one point he was hit on the head by a neighbour while trying to steal fence posts. As the neighbour testified: 'He wanted to run and was about to hit me with his axe, but I hit him with a stake so hard that blood starting coming from his nose and mouth.' This developed into a medical emergency, as the nearest doctor was 70 miles away. The neighbour was worried he had given Grishka permanent brain damage. Certainly Rasputin retained, for life, diabolic protuberances on his forehead. These were referred to, in several accounts, as 'bumps of budding horn'.

In 1891, aged 22, he was working for a Tobolsk haulier when he again mislaid his horse, claiming it had fallen in the river and drowned. He also lost a cartload of furs, which he insisted was stolen while he was relieving himself on the side of the road. The British chaplain in St Petersburg in the early 1900s, the Rev Bousfield Swan Lombard, wrote with disapproval of several randomly selected transgressions: 'He was guilty of... many crimes, horse stealing, perjury and the rape of a very young girl'.

During these roustabout years, Rasputin resembled Dostoyevsky's Dmitri Karamazov, a blustering innocent, repeatedly falling prey to drink and gypsy women. He might have preferred a comparison to Dmitri's gentler younger brother, the spiritual Alyosha: Rasputin loved to evoke the honey and flowers of Siberia. But he was not altogether ashamed of his youthful misdoings, readily incorporating them into his wondrous life story: 'I was dissatisfied... I turned to drink'; 'I was a drunkard and smoked tobacco but then I repented and just look what I made of myself.'

Endless floggings and prison sentences proved counter-productive. Grishka had discovered 'the joy of suffering and abuse'. It was not until 1897, when Rasputin was in his late twenties, that the authorities found an effective punishment: banishing him from Pokrovskoye and sending him to a monastery. He spent three weeks walking the 325 miles to the 40 churches of Verkhoturye, sleeping in barns on the way. His dissolute father had once vowed to visit Verkhoturye as a penance. Now his son would go in his place. Rasputin later grandly claimed an inner voice said: 'Take up the cross and follow me.'

Other accounts claim that he reached the monastery simply by chance, after giving lifts to a seminary student or a priest: the prospective passenger had been obliged to seek out his carter, Grishka, and finally unearthed him at home, in an armchair, snoring loudly.

The Verkhoturye Monastery was considered by some clerics to be pagan, housing sectarians of whom the regular Orthodox Church disapproved. The most extreme of these sectarians were known as khlysty and would whip each other: '*khlyst*' being the Russian for whip. The khlyst men were forever either testing their mettle by sharing beds with 'spiritual wives' and resisting temptation or throwing themselves into sadomasochistic orgies. Some preferred not to trust to their mettle and simply to castrate themselves.

At that time there were khlyst churches, 'arks', in 30 Russian provinces. Congregations, known as 'ships', would gather, wearing white 'tunics of fervour' and calling themselves Christs or Mothers of God. The founder of the movement had thrown all his books into the river, seeking instead the 'golden book of life' and instigating the worship of a Christ figure born to a woman and man both aged 100. Rasputin would presumably have chosen the golden book of life over real books. But he might not have been so keen on the ancient parents: his distaste for older women was matched by rage at his ageing father.

Rasputin spent three months at Verkhoturye, where it seems he was preyed upon by at least two over-excited monks. His first admirer, Father Josif, pressed a thigh against him during a visit to his cell: Grishka was obliged to pile furniture against the door to prevent further calls. Father Josif was then joined by a second admirer, Father Sergius; the pair pleaded together through the door: 'We want to love you.'

He did, however, meet one monk, Father Makari, who appealed to him. Father Makari had misbehaved in his early life. Now he lived in a tumble-down shed and slept on a mud floor; he ate almost nothing but black bread and wore chains to mortify his flesh. The British Embassy chaplain, the Rev Mr Lombard, wrote approvingly of a good influence on Rasputin, doubtless Makari, who 'talked to him about the brevity of life, the necessity of preparation for death and hideousness of sin and the means of achieving salvation'. The Rev Mr Lombard would not have been put off by tales of Makari's extreme devotion: he himself performed exorcisms and was a student of the occult.

Rasputin kept in touch with Makari for the rest of his life, at one point even persuading the Tsar to give him money. Makari's only indulgence was his poultry: deprived of human company, he would chat to his hens and chickens.

A new Grishka returned to Pokrovskoye having given up alcohol, tobacco and meat. His supporters claim he did not touch vodka for years. In years to come he developed an odd belief that carnivores were in some way blackened by meat; fish eaters, on the other hand, were lightened and might even acquire a halo. The reformed Rasputin appeared 'with dishevelled hair and no hat, singing and waving his arms, blazing with the fire of the zealous convert'. During church services, he swung his arms and made grimaces; he beat his head on the church floor until it bled and 'sang in an improper voice'. To the relief of many of the congregants, he began holding separate services in a hole dug under the family stable.

This increase in religious fervour did not dull his sex drive. He may have resisted some button-pulling at first, but, as a healthy married man of 28, he was not about to become celibate. He soon began practising a sort of khlyst-style fusion of sex and religion.

This process began, curiously, with his successful resistance to the charms of a woodcutter's wife. He had undergone a struggle after being 'made to feel the pressure of her breasts against his arms and neck in the small *izba*'. Leaving the woodcutter's house frustrated, his attention was caught by some birds which, he maintained, were singing love songs to each other. The birds offered an irresistible example of joy in love and, declaring that 'nature glorifies God and makes us joyful', he resolved never to pass up any future opportunity for sex.

As luck would have it, he promptly ran into three obliging women bathing nude in the river. His approving daughter, Maria, later wrote: 'They accepted his love-making one by one.' After the 'love feast', Rasputin claimed he was put into a meditative state: 'The Virgin smiled at him.' He was keen to spread the word, taking his joy in love a stage further, insisting: 'chastity is the sin of pride'. He initiated orgies around fires under the stables, merrily embracing what he referred to as 'mutual sin'.

In one account, a Mr Verintsew describes a religious ceremony and orgy conducted by Rasputin in the woods near Pokrovskoye. The worshippers dug a pit, which they filled with logs and leaves. Rasputin then lit a fire, offered prayers to St Michael and threw incense into the flames. The congregants held hands and began to dance; Rasputin prided himself on his dancing; he would leap and shout 'Oh', in the manner of someone lowered into icy water, then whirl in place for a whole hour at a time. If a dance had to go one way or the other, he made a point of dancing towards the left.

His daughter claimed that, when he heard songs such as 'Along the Roadway' and 'Troika, Fluffy Snow', he couldn't restrain himself. He would float about the room 'like a feather', with all the natural grace of Tolstoy's Natasha Rostov. Maria was delighted by her father's response to music: 'The rhythm of it made him vibrate as it does all primitive and sensitive people.' He himself had no reservations about dancing: 'David danced before the Ark of the Covenant.'

After dancing, the congregants, dizzy and overcome by 'spiritual beer', traditionally fell down. Then, as the embers of the fire were dying, they would turn to each other and have sex, or 'rejoice'. The *khlyst* leader, known as the pilot, would set the ball rolling, bearing down upon his female followers in a 'sweet smelling cloud'.

Mr Verintsew described how Rasputin, as pilot, descended on his female congregants, proclaiming: 'I cleanse you of all your sins.' Once the orgy was underway, wrote Mr Verintsew, the battle-cry was: 'Sin for salvation!' The correspondent for the *Daily Telegraph*, E.J. Dillon, later wrote wryly of Rasputin: 'The simple souls who gathered around him as their saviour were amazed at the ease with which they could qualify for the Kingdom of Heaven.'

While Mr Verintsew's vivid descriptions seem plausible enough, Maria's claim that her father dabbled in black magic seems less likely. She maintained that her father took part in black masses during which the Lord's Prayer was recited backwards and wine poured into the navel of a naked girl on the altar. In her accounts there is often a conflict between her love of her father and her weakness for sensationalism.

With his increasing influence, Grishka developed an unlikely taste for sophistry. He offered one miscreant in Pokrovskoye an unlikely prediction: 'You will attain the highest rank.' When the miscreant was hanged for murder, Grishka was challenged with the prediction. He replied with unexpected aplomb: 'I told you he'd be placed above everybody.'

The Pokrovskoye village priest, Father Peter, remained unimpressed. He had red hair and a red beard and apparently looked as though he was about to burst into flames. He complained to the Bishop of Tobolsk of Rasputin's practices. According to Maria, he was angry primarily because Rasputin was costing him money, taking services for which he himself was normally paid. But then Maria herself hated Father Peter because he had thumped her on the ear when she hadn't learnt her catechism.

It seemed now that for every new follower whose

soul Rasputin 'lightened', there was an ill-wisher lined up with Father Peter. Indeed, Yussoupov always maintained that, if Rasputin hadn't left Pokrovskoye, he would have ended up in the River Tura and nobody would have searched for him. Rasputin himself admitted: 'People blamed me when things went wrong, even if I had nothing to do with it.' But he later said confusingly: 'I spent my first 28 years in the world and I was one with it.'

So it was perhaps just as well that, in 1898, aged 29, Grigory Rasputin experienced a life-changing vision. He was taking a break, standing halfway down a furrow and leaning on his hoe, when the Virgin Mary appeared, hovering in the sky and pointing to the horizon. She wore a purple-brown veil and dress and looked, coincidentally, exactly like a statue of the Virgin in the Kazan Cathedral at St Petersburg. This vision was accompanied by the celestial voices of 1,000 angels. Whatever sceptics later made of the vision, Rasputin himself had no doubts, proudly marking the relevant furrow with a wooden cross.

That night he claimed he woke to find his icon of the Virgin Mary weeping and issuing silent instructions: 'Go, wander, and cleanse people of their sins.' At Verkhoturye, the ascetic Makari was very excited when he heard of the manifestations, telling Rasputin he must now walk thousands of miles to Mount Athos in Greece.

The family had mixed reactions when they heard of Rasputin's new calling. His wife, Praskovia, mindful of her husband's appetites, worried that there was 'something lacking in the way she responded to his love-making'. His father was equally convinced his son was simply skiving off the harvest. Rasputin failed to tell either of them when exactly he planned to leave; they only realised he'd gone when they noticed his robe and staff were missing.

It would take him a full ten months to reach Mount Athos. He would have been sporting a beard at this time, as Athos had laws forbidding entry to 'any woman, any female, any eunuch and anyone with smooth visage'. He was horrified to find monks openly engaged in homosexual activity and later complained to Makari that he'd seen monks ravaging a novice. He claimed that only one in a hundred pilgrims was following in the footsteps of Christ. He himself was proud of his privations, boasting peremptorily: 'Wore shackles for three years, was attacked by wolves, they did not harm me.' He claimed to have gone six months without changing his underwear or laying hands upon himself.

He entered into a routine. Every spring he would wander to holy places and return, perhaps conveniently, after the harvest. At one point he claimed to have walked to the Holy Land and, in the space of two and a half years, to have walked 7,000 miles. He would boast of his endurance: 'I didn't sleep for 40 nights each spring.' How much walking he actually did is impossible to know. It is tempting to imagine him walking to the next village and holing up in a bar until the harvest was safely over.

His patchy presence at home was, however, much prized by his young children, including the new baby, Varya. He took all three to fetes and retained sufficient energy after his pilgrimages to play ball games. His decision to teach Dmitri to drive the family cart proved unwise; aged 13, Dmitri tipped the cart over with 11-year-old Maria on board. Fortunately, both were unhurt. He relayed Russian fables, including the Dragonfly and the Ant, the Rich Man and the Cobbler and, perhaps most appropriately, the Poet and the Millionaire.

Praskovia never failed to welcome her constantly returning husband, falling to her knees in homage. This, despite his frequently being so bedraggled that she struggled to recognise him. She was not put out by his new habit of bringing back groups of young women in nun's clothes. It was around this time that his life-long love of unimaginative nicknames was spawned as he named these early followers: 'Hot Stuff', 'Boss Lady', 'Sexy Girl'. He made up equally leaden titles for the boys that he came across: 'Fella', 'Long Hair' or 'Big Breeches'.

There was the odd scandal, including a woman who claimed he had raped her in his cellar. But the doughty Praskovia took it all in her stride. Indeed, she convinced herself that sex was a burden for her Grishka. She was learning well: altruistic sin was one of her husband's favourite notions. He maintained that he generously took upon himself the sin of each of his sexual encounters and, further, that these sins reduced the overall amount in the world. Presumably he nodded his whiskery head sagely as Praskovia lamented: 'Each man must bear his cross and this is his.'

After more pressure from the irascible Father Peter, an inquiry into Rasputin's activities was launched in Pokrovskoye in 1903 by Bishop Anthony of Tobolsk. Rasputin never had any official role within the Church, but some of the Church leaders clearly felt that his spiritual activities fell under their jurisdiction. A policeman snuck into his services dressed as a peasant. Unfortunately for Father Peter, the inquiry foundered, as the policeman not only failed to find anything irregular, but succumbed to a full-blown attack of what would become known as '*Rasputinschina*'.

Rasputin was aged 33 when he decided he had had enough of rustic life and set out on a near-600-mile walk to the nearest city, Kazan. Or at least that is how it would appear. It is hard to tell how purposeful Rasputin actually was in many of the things he did in his life – to what extent he directed himself and to what extent his actions were dictated by random moods and circumstances.

It was in Kazan that he had his first taste of fine living, sitting in lavishly carpeted rooms, watching gentlefolk sip tea rather than suck it through sugar. His subsequent passion for gadgets was inspired by this first sight of radios, electric lights and, most importantly, telephones.

The telephone was to become a staple of Rasputin's life. In later years he would use the phone to vet women callers, asking how old they were and what they looked like, before making appointments. He and his daughter Maria became notorious for making nuisance calls. Maria would make suggestive overtures to men listed in the phone directory, while Rasputin enjoyed exposing bashful supporters when he knew they had company, waiting on the line with grim satisfaction, as the man-servant delivered the unwelcome news: 'I have Grishka Rasputin on the phone.' His happiest moments on the telephone, however, were spent dancing: a singer friend would run through a medley of songs while he clutched the receiver and danced in squats, twirls and stamps.

Shortly after his arrival in Kazan, Rasputin managed to gain the confidence of one particular cleric after warning him of a knife attack. But other clerics were not so impressed by his burgeoning love of the bathhouse. They heard that he was inviting women to wash his genitals: 'Take off your clothes and wash the *muzhik*' [peasant]. The women would watch as he, at least in theory, controlled himself; they would then thrash him with twigs. At one point he took two sisters, aged 15 and 20, for a thorough session of washing and thrashing. When he was accosted by their outraged mother, he pronounced grandly: 'Now you may feel at peace. The Day of Salvation has dawned for your daughters.' An accusation levelled at Rasputin by the Tobolsk Theological Consistory concerning his 'odd behaviour towards women' did nothing to dampen his ardour. Indeed, the joys of urban life took such a hold that he was soon

It was widely acknowledged that the Man of God's
eyes were mesmeric and that he could expand
and contract the pupils at will

gravitating from Kazan towards the larger city of Kiev.

In Kiev he had his first encounter with Russia's Imperial family. Grand Duchess Militza was married to the Tsar's cousin, Grand Duke Peter, and was the elder of two Montenegrin princesses, known as the 'Black Sisters' or 'Black Peril'. She considered herself a religious expert and in the early 1900s was the proud author of 'Selected Passages from the Holy Fathers'.

Intrigued by tales of Rasputin's powers, Militza, then visiting Kiev, tracked him down to an obscure shed, where she found him sawing wood. She and her younger sister, Princess Anastasia, had once been considered great beauties at Court. Militza retained a soulful face, with large, dark, sorrowful eyes and a delicate mouth, but by this time she was well into her thirties and evidently held no interest for Rasputin. Though aware of her presence, he carried on sawing noisily. She told him to sit down but he refused; when she asked how long he would remain in Kiev, he replied curtly that God would tell him when he should leave. His abrasiveness and her conciliatory responses would become characteristic of Rasputin's exchanges with members of the aristocracy, who were prone to welcome his rudeness as a mark of integrity.

Their second meeting was altogether happier. Rasputin had arrived in the Russian capital, St Petersburg, in 1903. His unlikely claim was that he had come to raise money for the church at Pokrovskoye. Whatever was behind his motivations, he seems to have decided, at this point, that it might be worth being civil to grand duchesses after all. He paid a visit to Militza and her

The Montenegrin Princesses Anastasia and Mil-
itza, with a tambourine, circa 1890. The Black Peril, as
they became known, were considered great beauties.

younger 'black sister', Anastasia. Completing a formidable party would be the Tsar's so-called 'dread uncle', Grand Duke Nicholas.

It emerged, during the visit, that Anastasia was consumed with worry about her dog: vets had given him barely two months to live and he was breathing heavily. Tea was postponed while Rasputin put his hand on the dog's head, shut his eyes and prayed for a good half-hour. When the dog's breathing improved, the Grand Duke stepped forward jubilantly, but was brazenly waved away. By the end of the prayer, the dog was restored to health and keen to lick his healer's well-seasoned hand. Rasputin issued a bald pronouncement, which would, in fact, prove accurate: 'He will live for some years.'

Years later, when Rasputin's wife, Praskovia, needed a hysterectomy, the grateful Grand Duke Nicholas paid for the best surgeons in St Petersburg. Praskovia had woken in the night, screaming with pain, thinking that she was suffering from cramps. She had then collapsed while working in the fields. Her husband, by that time fully immersed in the comforts of Court life, may have felt twinges of guilt as he made the six-day journey back to Pokrovskoye to pick her up.

After the operation, Rasputin treated her to a *drozhky* ride around the sights, including the Peter and Paul Fortress and the Winter Palace. But Praskovia was not impressed: 'I don't want to live here,' she proclaimed, before taking the first train available back to Tyumen. Rasputin's father, Efim, had been equally underwhelmed by St Petersburg: upon his arrival, he made the sign of the cross, and left the city within a week.

It was during these early days in the capital that Rasputin met the man who would become one of his most unhinged followers, the monk Iliodor. A celebrated anti-semite, Iliodor led processions carrying giant dolls dressed in Jewish kaftans. At the end of rumbustious ceremonies, the dolls would be burnt. Iliodor was 11 years Rasputin's junior, but, when they met, it was Rasputin who acted like an awe-struck child, putting the grimy fingers of one hand in his mouth and stamping his feet on the spot, as if about to gallop away.

Despite this inauspicious start, the bearded pair became friends, spending days fishing on the Tura. Maria offers a slightly unconvincing picture of them casting their lines while enjoying 'interminable religious arguments and philosophical discussions'.

Meanwhile, bishops in St Petersburg gathered to listen to Rasputin's largely predictable prophecies: one bishop would suffer a hernia, another would lose his mother. A third prediction, that one would father a child out of wedlock, was obviously more outlandish. It is not known how the bishops regarded the finer details of the predictions, but they were generally impressed. Father John of Kronstadt, the highly respected priest who had heard the last confession of Tsar Nicholas's father, Alexander III, interrupted one of his services to proclaim: 'We have a Man of God in our congregation. Step forward.' Grigory Rasputin leapt forward. He would probably have enjoyed the khlyst-like flavour of Father John's services, during which the congregation were encouraged to shout their sins.

Rasputin's reputation was gathering steam. Reports from the secret police, the Okhrana, echoed the enthusiastic clerics, claiming that Rasputin could blow on a handful of earth and turn it into a magnificent rose tree. Hundreds of women crowded outside the house where he was staying and a St Petersburg paper reported that he 'restored sight to the blind and movements to the paralysed'. When the occasional question arose about his activities at the bath-house, his friend Iliodor would defend him, supporting newspaper reports that he 'visits bathing establishments and brings holy word to those who bathe... They are morally cleansed.'

The Tsar and Tsarina's own confessor, Bishop Feofan, was one of Rasputin's most assiduous early supporters. Feofan was a particularly valuable ally: along with his connections at Court, he was known to be associated with the St Petersburg Theological Academy. Feofan's credentials could not be faulted, but his endorsement of Rasputin never represented any kind of approval from the Church. The handful of bishops now supporting Rasputin were out on a limb.

Feofan testified at the 1917 Commission that Rasputin had originally arrived with a letter from a Bishop Chrysanthos. 'Once he [another bishop, Sergius] invited us to his lodgings for tea, and introduced for the first time to me and several monks and seminarians a recently arrived Man of God, Brother Grigory as we

The Tsarina's unswerving devotion to her husband, 'beloved Nicky dear' is laid bare in a torrent of passionate love letters. Unfortunately her devotion was inflamed by a protective, motherly impulse; she believed herself smarter than he.

called him then. He amazed us all with his psychological perspicacity.' They quizzed him about the fate of a squadron due to engage in a battle with the Japanese. Rasputin was pessimistic: 'I feel in my heart it will be sunk.' He proved correct.

Bishop Feofan related how Brother Grigory had gone to Sarov, in 1903, to attend a canonisation, and announced to the congregation that the long-awaited heir to the throne would be born within a year. The prophecy was borne out when, following the births of four grand duchesses, the Tsarevich Alexis was born on August 12 1904. Feofan believed that he had been the one who had told Grand Duchess Militza about Rasputin: 'I let slip that a Man of God was among us named Grigory Rasputin.' But Grand Duchess Militza had, of course, already shared tea with Rasputin following their less productive exchange over the wood-saw in Kiev.

Such was the trust between Bishop Feofan and Brother Grigory that, at one point, they lived together. It was Grand Duchess Militza who orchestrated Rasputin's move into Feofan's house, but Rasputin soon found the set-up constraining. He disliked limits on his movements or, more importantly, limits on visits from 'little ladies' and soon transferred himself to the house of a less scrupulous journalist friend. He would eventually move into flats of his own on the English Prospect and then on Nikolaevsky Street.

But Feofan remained happily ignorant of the foibles of his Man of God. Like Iliodor, he was ready with explanations of the trips to the Kazan bath-houses: 'He too wanted to test himself, to see if he had extinguished passion in himself.' Nobody would argue with the sainted Feofan when he insisted, even more implausibly, that Rasputin had mastery over the weather. This particular rumour had begun in Pokrovskoye after Rasputin had been assailed by angry fathers and husbands of 'Rasputinki'. He had raised his arm to the sky at the beginning of a long, dry spell and said: 'Let there be no rain for three months.'

The Bishop never tired of singing his Man of God's praises to the Tsar and Tsarina: 'It is the voice of the Russian soil which speaks through him.' He added that Rasputin had 'so deep a passion of repentance that I would all but guarantee his eternal salvation'.

On November 1 1905, two weeks after signing the October Manifesto outlining Russia's first parliament, the Tsar and Tsarina agreed to have tea with Rasputin. The tea was held on a sunny afternoon, at the Montenegrin Black Princesses' villa, Sergevka, at Peterhof. Brother Grigory was immediately relaxed, addressing the Imperial couple as Batiushka and Matiushka (little father and little mother). He would soon refer to them even more simply as 'Papa' and 'Mama'. The Tsar made a characteristically unforthcoming entry in his diary: 'We had tea with Militza and Stana [Anastasia]. We met the Man of God Grigory from the province of Tobol.'

Rasputin was not the first mystic at Court. Holy Men had always been a feature of Court life. In the early

1800s the Holy Man to Nicholas I had accurately predicted the sequence of names of future monarchs, concluding, ominously, that Nicholas II would be followed by a 'peasant with an axe in his hand'.

The vacillating Tsar Nicholas II frequently summoned clairvoyants to conjure up the spirit of his domineering father, Alexander III, who twisted forks in knots and called him 'girlie'. Alexander clearly retained some influence over his son, and Nicholas was a willing subject, refusing to be put off, even when his late father's guidance was at its most vague. One medium, a bogus gynaecologist, passed on a typical message: 'Take courage, my son, and do not abandon the struggle.' This same medium insisted that a catastrophe in Russia could only be averted while he himself was alive. He was sadly vindicated, dying just five months before the Revolution.

Another of the Tsar's peasant clairvoyants correctly foretold the disastrous outcome of the Russo-Japanese War and disconcerted the Tsar by banging dolls and shouting 'Sergei'. He later insisted she was referring to Grand Duke Sergei, who was blown up by terrorists in 1905. While he consulted clairvoyants, the Tsarina and her friend Anna Vyrubova were said to be obsessed by scrutinising Egyptian cards and reading coffee grounds.

The couple's Court priest, Father Vassiliev, was himself no stranger to mysticism. The Tsarina maintained that his religious fervour made him 'shriek and hop like a dervish'. His favourite homily seemed unhelpful: 'Don't worry, the devil neither smokes nor drinks nor engages in revelry and yet he is the devil.'

Grand Duchess Militza recognised fertile ground and took it upon herself to introduce a series of holy fools to the Imperial couple. First there was Matryona the Barefoot, dressed in rags, who brought icons to the Palace and shouted incomprehensible prophecies. She was followed by an epileptic called Mitya Kobalya from Kozelsk, who, like Rasputin, came with the endorsement of Bishop Feofan. Mitya had short arms and spoke as unintelligibly as Matryona. However, he had the advantage of an interpreter, a sexton called Egorov. Mitya looked the part: 'He wears his hair long and unbound and goes about barefoot the year round, leaning on a staff' was the way one onlooker described him. He predicted Russia's defeat at Port Arthur. He was on less certain ground, however, when asked, years before, whether the Tsarina would bear an heir. The Tsarina herself had put the question to him; Mitya's response had been to scream so loudly that she had hysterics. The translator's barely audible interpretation was that it was 'too early to tell'.

'Blessed Mitya' must have been a controversial presence, as Anna Vyrubova later tried to claim that he had never been to the Palace. But on January 14 1906 the Tsar referred to an exhaustingly long meeting with Mitya in his diary: 'The Man of God Dmitri came to see us from Kozelsk near the Optina Pustyn Monastery. He brought with him an image drawn according to a vision he had had. We talked for about an hour and a half.'

If members of the Imperial entourage had misgivings about this particular Man of God, Mitya certainly enjoyed the blessing of another unconventional character at Court, a Tibetan healer called Peter Badmaev. The healer, subsequently accused of drugging the Tsar, insisted that Mitya 'impressed me as an intelligent, religious peasant'. But Badmaev's attempts, over two years, to treat Mitya's catarrh were unsuccessful; the Man of God never shook off another of his sobriquets, Mitya the Nasal-voiced. Incidentally, Rasputin mistrusted Dr Badmaev: 'That Chinaman would betray you for a kopeck.'

The best known of Rasputin's predecessors at the Court, however, was a French butcher – some said hairdresser – called M. Philippe Nizier-Vachod. He had been expelled from a college where he was studying medicine, and had then taken it upon himself to treat patients with what he referred to as 'psychic fluids and astral forces'. He claimed to live on the borderline between two worlds. The French authorities set no store by his remedies: he was arrested five times for practising medicine without a licence.

The Black Peril, Militza and Anastasia, had met M. Philippe in Cannes. In a great state of excitement, Militza reported back to the Tsarina that this new mystic could cure all diseases, including syphilis. She introduced the Tsar and Tsarina to M. Philippe when he followed the sisters back to Russia. According to some sources, the Tsar met M. Philippe during a visit to France. One of the Tsar's grand duke cousins was horrified, insisting that M. Philippe had a 'terrible southern French accent'. He added, in further disapproval, that the Tsar and Tsarina would return from sessions with M. Philippe, having 'fallen into a mystical frame of mind'.

M. Philippe was also able to summon the tireless spirit of Tsar Alexander III and apparently shared Rasputin's mastery of the weather, once tempering a storm to protect the Imperial yacht, the *Standart*. He even boasted that he could make himself and others invisible. On one occasion, Prince Yussoupov's father waved at Grand Duchess Militza as he spotted her riding in a carriage with M. Philippe but she failed to wave back. When he later challenged her, she replied that he couldn't possibly have seen her: M.Philippe had been wearing a hat that made his companion invisible.

Of prime importance to the Imperial couple was M. Philippe's claim to be able to determine the sex of an unborn baby through the 'transcendental practice of hermetic medicine, astronomy and psychurgy'. Sadly, his fallibility in this direction was exposed when the Tsarina gave birth to her fourth daughter, Anastasia, in June 1901, rather than the predicted son. Upon the baby's arrival, M. Philippe ungraciously accused the Tsarina of having insufficient faith. As the matter of an heir became more urgent, it was said that he installed himself in the Tsar and Tsarina's bedroom. His capacity to make himself invisible would have proven invaluable.

Aware of M. Philippe's growing band of critics, the Tsar and Tsarina began calling him, cryptically, 'our Friend', as they would later do with Rasputin. The Tsar made several vain attempts to protect him: at one point requesting a medical diploma from the French Government. He finally gave M. Philippe a cursory title: 'Inspector of port sanitary services'.

But the disapproving Grand Duke was not to be appeased, noting: 'The bad thing is that they cover their visits to Znamenka [Militza's palace] in secrecy.' The Tsar's mother, the down-to-earth Dowager, became so anxious about M. Philippe that she sent secret agents to France to investigate his background. She need not have worried. M. Philippe's days at the Russian Court were, by then, already numbered. The turning point had come when the Tsarina, carried away by M. Philippe's pronouncements, fell victim to a phantom pregnancy. It was believed that M. Philippe had hypnotised her; there were wilder rumours that she had given birth to a monster. Before M.Philippe was dispatched back to Lyon, he correctly predicted that the Tsar and Tsarina would one day have another 'Friend'. He left the Tsarina an icon with a bell which he said would ring at the approach of enemies. He had one final success, prophesying the date on which he would die, in 1905. When the excitable younger Montenegrin Princess, Anastasia, heard of his death, she proclaimed that his spirit had entered her body.

For all the Black Sisters' attachment to their previous men of God, they were particularly possessive of Rasputin. They had, after all, hosted the momentous tea at which Rasputin had first been presented to 'the Tsars'. After that meeting, Militza had made Rasputin swear not to contact the Palace without consulting her. If he did, she warned obscurely, it would be the end of him. She may have been worried about future fallings-out: relations between her and the Tsarina had already cooled since the days when the Black Princesses had been in charge of emptying the Imperial chamber pot.

But Bishop Feofan was later to testify that his irrepressible protégé cared nothing for Militza's warnings. Within a few months, Rasputin had contacted the Tsar independently and made several visits to the Palace with Feofan: three years after his encounter with Grand Duchess Militza in the woodshed, the mercurial Rasputin was developing a taste for high society.

On July 18 1906, Rasputin enjoyed his second tea with the Tsar and Tsarina. He had written a sparse telegram: 'Tsar father, I want to bring you an icon of Righteous St Simon of Verkhoturye.' He brought each of the four young Grand Duchesses and the two-year-old Tsarevich an icon and a piece of consecrated bread. It was said that he challenged the Tsarina to lift a box of matches, having persuaded her that it weighed three tons. The impressionable Tsarina, unsurprisingly, failed to lift it.

He returned to the Alexander Palace, on Friday October 12, and spoke to the Tsar and Tsarina at some length. The Tsar wrote enthusiastically to his most powerful minister, Peter Stolypin, saying that Rasputin 'made a strong impression on Her Majesty and me – our conversation lasted well over an hour.' The Tsar suggested Rasputin visit Stolypin's daughter, who had lost a leg in a bomb attack. Stolypin agreed to allow Rasputin to give his daughter a blessing. But he remained grimly unconvinced by Anna Vyrubova's claim that his daughter benefited from any kind of healing.

One of the Tsar's earliest favours to Brother Grigory was to allow him to change his name to Rasputin Novy – Rasputin had always wanted to distance himself from the association his name had with the word for debauchee, '*rasputnik*'. The request was granted in a record-breaking seven days, on December 22 1906. Later Rasputin would claim it was the little Tsarevich Alexis who had christened him 'new', having clapped his hands and greeted him with the shout '*novy, novy*'.

In fact, throughout his life, Rasputin was usually referred to as Brother or Father Grigory by his supporters; 'the Tsars' called him, simply, Grigory. Feofan would certainly have introduced him into society as Brother Grigory. His early encounters with the aristocracy included evenings at the home of a Countess Ignatiev. Fortunately for Rasputin, the Countess's salon was known for its outlandish guests as much as for its celebration of the autocratic principle. Next to the barefoot, screaming 'Blessed Mitya', Rasputin would have seemed eminently presentable.

But his most important new connection was the Tsarina's friend, Anna Vyrubova. She first encountered the Man of God on a train, when, true to form, he had asked her about her 'unhappy' life. The train carriage did not lend itself to any exchange of confidences; Anna was prevented from filling in the sorry details until the pair had been formally introduced at Militza's palace. But then she poured out her worries about her impending marriage, due to take place in 15 days' time. She had misgivings about her groom, who would, indeed, turn out to be a deranged alcoholic sadist. At this late stage,

Anna was still wondering whether to go ahead with the wedding. Rasputin's predictions were unhelpful: 'He [Rasputin] told me I should marry but the union will be unhappy.'

It was later rumoured that Anna's husband was maddened after finding her in bed with the Tsarina: the two women were believed to enjoy an 'unnatural friendship'. Anna was certainly devoted, convinced that the Tsarina had once cured her with the touch of a hand. But the Tsarina, for her part, does not seem to have been so enamoured, once describing her friend as encumbered with 'stomach and legs colossal'. She added that Anna had an unappealing habit of speaking 'as if she had a mouthful of porridge'. In fact, contrary to any rumours, Anna remained bemused about sex, flatly refusing conjugal relations with her new husband and lamenting to the young Maria Rasputin: 'I hear of those who enjoy it so much. I wish I could.'

Over the next ten years, Anna's passion would be directed towards Rasputin. Gleb Botkin, the son of the Tsar's doctor, believed her the victim of 'sexual hysteria and religious mania...' and that she was 'head over heels in love with Rasputin'. She was thrilled by his divergent personalities – the 'peasant with an unkempt beard'; the 'Saint who uttered Heaven-inspired words'. When he held her hand she is said to have moaned and trembled.

It is not known what Rasputin thought of her in these early days. She was young, in her early twenties, but the Tsarina was not the only one to note her less attractive features. Yussoupov said she had a 'puffy shiny face and no charm whatsoever'. The French Ambassador, Maurice Paleologue, dismissed her as: 'rather stout... with an ample build... a fat neck and full fleshy lips'. Either way, Rasputin made full use of the fox fur which she gave him to put on his bed in St Petersburg. At one point, he suggested provocatively that she watch while he was soaped by his wife in the bath-house at Pokrovskoye.

In any case, by the time of the Revolution, there were so many rumours linking Anna Vyrubova to Rasputin that she finally decided to have herself officially examined by doctors. The result, which she promptly made public, was perhaps unsurprising: she was still a virgin.

What was Rasputin's appeal for the Imperial couple? Both loved the idea of the adoring peasant. The Tsar had a distaste for sophistication, making the same grimace when saying 'intelligentsia' as when he said 'syphilis'. Reverence for the peasant was rife within the Russian aristocracy of the time. Many had taken up Count Tolstoy's view that the peasants were 'closer to God... They lead moral working lives and their simple wisdom is in many ways superior to all the artifices of our culture and philosophy.'

The Tsarina liked to attend public churches with the ever-obliging Anna Vyrubova in order to be with 'plain people'. 'The peasants love us,' she insisted.

Amid the fripperies of life at Court, there was always a call for an uncorrupted straight-talker, a character like Queen Victoria's John Brown. Indeed, one of the Imperial family's closest companions, Lili Dehn, compared the Tsarina's faith in Rasputin to Queen Victoria's in Mr Brown. Inevitably the Tsarina's worship of the peasants was encouraged by Rasputin who claimed: 'Great is the peasant in the eyes of God.'

Rasputin manifested all the right, 'plain' attributes; he also had good timing. By late 1905, the Imperial Couple were suffering the effects of several bouts of civil unrest and the tragedy of Bloody Sunday, in which the Tsar's soldiers had shot dead hundreds of innocent demonstrators. They were increasingly taking refuge in the Alexander Palace in Tsarskoye Selo, 15 miles from the capital.

The Tsarina had always been unpopular with the Russian aristocracy. She deemed them decadent, while they dismissed her in turn as haughty and puritanical. She had no time for creature comforts, existing happily on chicken cutlets twice a day for months on end.

The Tsar, meanwhile, was considered a colourless and indecisive character. He was ripe for moulding and cheerfully went along with his wife as she indulged her oddly conflicted appetites for the bourgeois and the spiritual. The Tsarina was as happy ordering chintzes from the latest Maples catalogue as she was cultivating mystics.

Hated by the revolutionaries and mistrusted by the aristocracy, the Imperial couple became ever more isolated. A *folie à deux* extended to a *folie à sept* as the five children followed their mother's lead in gravitating towards 'plain' Russians and outlandish prophets. Rasputin, the peasant Man of God, seemed like the answer to a family prayer. The increasingly friendless Imperial Family had found someone they could call, once again, 'our Friend'.

As opposition to Rasputin's presence at Court grew within the Orthodox Church, the Government and even among the Russian people, the Imperial couple took the criticism personally. The more vicious the attacks, the more they would be seen, particularly by the Tsarina, as tests of faith, to be withstood at any price.

The Palace guards labelled Rasputin a 'peasant of modest allure'. But for the Tsarina there was nothing modest about it. If she was drawn, first, to his obvious plainness, she was soon enslaved by his apparent healing powers. In the course of the next few years, he seemed to prove himself the only one able to cure her beloved son.

Arguments have raged as to whether Rasputin actually possessed healing powers at all; if they existed, what form did they take? The Tsar's mother, his brother-in-law, the Grand Duke Alexander, and the children's French tutor, Pierre Gilliard, deemed his cures nothing more than coincidence. Others, including Alexis's English tutor, Sydney Gibbes, put them down to hypnosis: the writer Robert K. Massie, the author of *Nicholas and Alexandra*, who himself had a haemophiliac son, is one of those who believe that hypnosis can help stem bleeding.

It was suggested that Rasputin's ability to comfort the Tsarina may have had a calming effect on her son:

if his blood pressure dropped, the bleeding could have eased. One of Rasputin's secrets might have been his distaste for the wonder drug aspirin, available from 1899. With all his love of novelty, Rasputin distrusted aspirin. He was right to be suspicious: aspirin, then being dished out by the Court doctors for pain relief, was later discovered to be an anti-coagulant; the pills would have made the bleeding considerably worse. Rasputin once claimed that Alexis would be mysteriously cured by the time he was 13. But haemophilia is still incurable.

Whatever lay behind the cures, the courtiers had to acknowledge their effectiveness. Even the sceptical Director of the Imperial Court, Alexander Mossolov, wrote of Rasputin's 'incontestable success in healing'.

Alexis was aged three when he was first healed by Rasputin. He had fallen in the grounds of the Palace; he had hurt his leg and his face was so badly swollen that his eyes had closed. He had been ill for three days before the Man of God was summoned and appeared in his bedroom. After several minutes of silent prayer, the boy smiled and his mother cried with joy. Rasputin silenced the ecstatic Tsarina with the same gesture with which he had rebuffed the dog-loving Grand Duke Nicholas four years earlier.

On another occasion, it was said, Rasputin was talking to the Tsarina about providence when he suddenly interrupted himself, shouting: 'He's in the blue room.' The pair ran to the blue billiard room, to find Alexis standing on the table. Rasputin scooped the boy up seconds before the table was hit by a huge, falling chandelier. Of such stuff are legends created.

Rasputin's visits to the Palace, dressed, according to one unlikely report, in 'thick black glasses and a cossack uniform' became increasingly frequent. Unfortunately, in these early days, it was deemed crucial to keep the boy's illness secret, even from his tutors. This meant that nobody outside the immediate family would have been aware of the poignant reason behind the visits. The Tsar's own sister, Grand Duchess Xenia, reported that she knew nothing of Alexis's haemophilia until the spring of 1912, by which time the boy was nearly eight.

The reasons behind Rasputin's uncharacteristic discretion cannot be known. Did he fail to grasp the significance of the boy's illness? Was he simply being considerate towards the Tsar and Tsarina? The most likely explanation is that he believed it in his own interests to be discreet, though this was not always enough to silence him.

The Court doctors did, of course, understand the reasons behind Rasputin's presence. But their understanding did not make the visits any less irksome to them. The blow to their professional pride was exacerbated by Brother Grigory's lack of social graces. This despite at least one of the doctors barely cutting the mustard himself. As Gleb Botkin sniffed of Dr Derevenko: 'He was... of peasant stock and showed it only too clearly in his manners and speech.' The smarter Dr Botkin was frequently involved in slanging matches with Rasputin: Botkin baited him by insisting he had performed autopsies and never found a soul, while Rasputin retorted snappily: 'How many emotions, memories, imagination have you found?'

In a misjudged bid to improve relations, Rasputin once visited Dr Botkin at his house in Tsarskoye Selo. He pretended to have some interesting medical complaint but was shown the door, with Dr Botkin's words ringing in his ears: 'I can see you're as fit and healthy as a bull.' Whenever they subsequently passed each other in a corridor, Dr Botkin would turn his back.

For all the fervent support he enjoyed within the immediate Imperial family, Rasputin's position at Court was ever more precarious. The younger of the Tsar's sisters, Grand Duchess Olga, who first saw him when he was visiting the Imperial children, had initially been chary of Rasputin, but was then impressed by how relaxed Alexis was with him, jumping about and pretending to be a rabbit. She was completely won over after seeing him praying with the children: 'I was conscious of the man's sincerity.'

But her approval was short-lived. Within months he had offended her by snuggling up to her on a sofa, putting his arm around her shoulder, stroking her and asking if she was happy and loved her husband. The Grand Duchess, who was in fact not happy with her husband, reacted badly, finding his curiosity 'unbridled and embarrassing'.

While Mossolov, the Director of the Imperial Court, acknowledged Rasputin's healing powers, he never got over his initial dislike. He described Rasputin as having 'an impudent familiarity combined with a servility which fitted like a glove on this upstart'. His low opinion was formed after their first meeting, at the Hotel d'Europe, when Rasputin disgraced himself, in some appalling but unspecified way: 'As he left he ruined my overcoat.'

The pair's subsequent meetings did nothing to change Mossolov's view. He was particularly horrified to discover that 'our Friend' ate exclusively with his fingers: 'Rasputin set to, without knife or fork.'

Grand Duchess Militza turned against her protégé when she found he had been visiting the Palace secretly: 'You, Grigory, are an underhanded person,' she raged. The Black Sisters would have been even more disconcerted by the silence of the Imperial couple. Through lengthy discussions about Rasputin, no mention had been made of any visits. As the Tsar wrote in his diary, December 9 1906: 'Militza and Stana [Anastasia] dined with us – discussed Grigory all evening.'

Militza became involved in a pamphlet accusing Rasputin of the 'Spreading of False Khlystlike Doctrine and of Forming a Society of Followers of His False Doctrine'. In the pamphlet, released on September 6 1907, Rasputin was accused of 'self-importance and Satanic pride'. If it could now be established that he was a *khlyst*, he could be excommunicated. Rasputin's old enemy, Bishop Anthony of Tobolsk, sprang into action, demanding monthly bulletins from three local priests in Pokrovskoye.

asputin made a habit of returning regularly to Pokrovskoye: 'I came home joyful,' he would proclaim. Ongoing home improvements may well have contributed to his joy. Through her early years of devotion, Grand Duchess Militza had showered the Rasputins with money, allowing them to move from the old *izba* to a lavish two-storey wooden house, with flower boxes in the windows and a tin roof. Further funds had been found for upper guest rooms, duly kitted out with a large floor clock and an Offenbach piano. Rasputin was particularly keen on a new gramophone; he could now squat and stamp to an endless supply of rousing dance music.

If Rasputin felt any unease about falling out with his benefactor, he did not let it cramp his style. He carried on returning to his lavish house accompanied by a bevy of 'little ladies'. Praskovia still fell to her knees, removed his boots and marvelled at his growing wardrobe of silk shirts and smart sashes.

At the bidding of Bishop Anthony, the priests quizzed villagers about Rasputin's habits. But his neighbours were reluctant to testify against him, conceding only that he wore a gold pectoral cross and that strange music could be heard coming from his cellar. They admitted seeing him emerging, wet, from the bath-house, with women. But they seemed unfazed by this. He himself said cheerily: 'The sovereign knows... I don't go with one person but... with company.' Why shouldn't he 'hug and kiss little ladies'? The village children approved of him: 'Granddaddy Grishka' always had his pockets full of gumdrops and honey cakes.

In the end, the vague conclusion to the Bishop's elaborate inquiry in Pokrovskoye was that Rasputin had created some sort of religious society which held meetings for prayers. The villagers' refusal to condemn Rasputin may well have been connected with his largesse. As his influence and status rose at Court, so did his ability to bestow riches upon his home village. By this time he was providing horses, cows and even houses for poorer families. At one point he was given 5,000 roubles by the Tsar for the church. This, in fact, gave rise to an argument as the villagers declared that they preferred to spend the money on a school. Rasputin was frequently incensed by what he regarded as their lack of grace, flouncing off to Tyumen: 'Nobody understands a thing in this village.'

When troubling stories of Rasputin's habits began spreading in St Petersburg, the Tsarina decided to send Bishop Feofan to Pokrovskoye with her protégé, believing that the Bishop would return with glorious stories of Rasputin in his 'plain' element. She had been delighted by Anna Vyrubova's report of her trip to Pokrovskoye, during which villagers visited in the evening to sing, pray and share simple fare: 'raisins, bread, nuts and perhaps a bit of pastry.'

Feofan's more discerning party included the ascetic Father Makari, who might have been relieved to take a break from his mud hut and chickens. What Makari made of Rasputin's comfortable way of life can only be imagined, but Feofan was disgusted. His impression was that the house reflected a: 'semi-indigent peasant notion of how rich people lived in the cities'. Feofan disapproved of the wide beds with soft springy mattresses and was especially struck by the 'large soft carpet covering the entire floor'. He said finally that during a fast 'Brother Grigory ordered something to eat and cracked nuts'.

Rasputin was particularly shameless on his home turf: 'It cost 600 roubles', he announced, of an elaborate chandelier. Picking up a gold cross, he enthused: 'See this cross, it's got "N" stamped on it. The Tsar gave it – did it to honour me'. He would flourish jewelled eggs and icons and finally his prized silk shirts: 'Her Majesty sewed this for me'. One shirt had a missing collar: 'I gave it to "Papa" [the Tsar] to wear at night because he had a sore throat', he boasted. When his unhinged friend, the monk Iliodor, visited Pokrovskoye, Rasputin bragged that the Tsar had proclaimed him 'a true Christ... Me!'

It was this kind of behaviour that made Iliodor and his other fervent supporter Bishop Feofan begin to have second thoughts. But Rasputin seemed oblivious to their changes of heart. His behaviour rarely bore out his supporters' claim that he had learnt to 'read people' on his pilgrimages or that he could smell out enemies. Maria made efforts to explain her father's lack of acuity: 'He had an immediate, infallible instinct about people – then forgot it'.

With the increasingly wary Iliodor, Rasputin made the serious error of brandishing a stash of adoring letters from the Tsarina and the Grand Duchesses. In a cavalier mood, he left the letters lying around, and the sly Iliodor couldn't resist pocketing them.

The smart house in Pokrovskoye which Rasputin occupied intermittently from the early 1900s until his death. The house and its lavish furnishings were largely gifts from the Grand Duchess Militza.

Above: Rasputin with followers in Pokrovskoye
Below: With Maria, Varya and Dmitri

After his stay, Iliodor claimed that two of Rasputin's servants had tried to get into bed with him. Rasputin, in turn, accused Iliodor of ogling his devoted maid, Dounia, while she undressed for a wash. Despite their arguments, at the end of 1909 Rasputin accompanied Iliodor to his home town of Tsaritzyn. Here he blotted his copy book by failing to cure a holy fool called Nastya, who threw the contents of a chamber pot at him. But he had more success with other inhabitants and, when he left, was presented with a 160-rouble tea set.

If Rasputin could shrug off the misgivings of Feofan and Iliodor, he soon found himself facing an altogether fiercer enemy: the bullet-headed Peter Stolypin, Prime Minister and Minister of the Interior. Stolypin had not been impressed by the Tsar's fulsome letter to him about Rasputin in 1906. He set no store by the Man of God's attempt to help his daughter and was outraged when Rasputin tried to hypnotise him.

Ignorant of the most important reason for Rasputin's visits to the Palace, Stolypin thought he could simply use his powers of persuasion to keep the Man of God at bay. He succeeded in making the malleable Tsar promise, in 1908, to stop seeing Rasputin, but within weeks the Tsar had broken his word.

In desperation, Stolypin decided to ban Rasputin from St Petersburg for five years. But when attempts were made to pin the banning notice on him, Rasputin could not be found. He had, in fact, taken temporary refuge at his enemy Grand Duchess Militza's house, where he would have had an uncomfortable time of it.

Visits from her sister, Anastasia, may have been some consolation: Rasputin was in good odour with Anastasia after giving his blessing to her unpopular second marriage to the towering Grand Duke Nicholas. Now both Black Sisters were married to Romanov brothers, Peter and Nicholas. 'The marriage of the brother [Nicholas] will be the salvation of Russia,' gushed Rasputin.

But he would later change his mind about the marriage, making enemies of both Black Sisters. They in turn would go to the palace in Tsarskoye Selo to complain about Rasputin to the Tsarina, who received them coolly, discounting their tales out of hand.

Years later, in 1911, Stolypin would put together a damning report on Rasputin, but the Tsar simply threw it into the fire. He refused to discuss the subject: 'I can do nothing about it.' He gave a clue to the nature of his hesitation with one overheard remark: 'Better one Rasputin than ten fits of hysterics a day.' Rasputin was not comforted when he heard of the Tsar's stand against Stolypin. Instead, he growled to Anna Vyrubova that the Prime Minister still had too much power. But it turned out that, during these early days of Rasputin's rise, Stolypin actually had very little power. The Man of God's visits to Tsarskoye Selo carried on continuously through 1908 and 1909.

Though 'the Tsars' never granted Rasputin the ultimate honour of kissing his hand, they would readily peck a hairy cheek. The Tsarina frequently received

Brother Grigory at Anna Vyrubova's house, the 'portico to power', as Protopopov called it. She would enter followed by a footman with cakes and sandwiches. Yussoupov later wrote that Anna Vyrubova, as hostess, was 'intoxicated with playing the role of an influential person'. By the end of 1908 the Tsar was writing appreciatively in his diary that Rasputin had helped decorate Anna's Christmas tree.

Throughout 1909, the Tsar makes references to Rasputin's visits in his diary: '4 February... At 6.00 o'clock the Archimandrate Feofan and Grigory came to see us. He also saw the children.' '29 February... At 2.30 Grigory came to see us, and we received him with all the children. It was so good to hear him with the whole family.' '29 March (the Day of Christ's Joyful Resurrection)... After tea upstairs in the nursery I sat for a while with Grigory, who had come unexpectedly.' '26 April... From 6.00 to 7.00 we saw... Grigory... I also sat with Grigory a little while in the nursery this evening.' On August 15 1909, he wrote: 'I talked with Grigory a long time this evening.'

But for all the Tsar's buoyant diary entries, the Imperial couple recognised the growing opprobrium attached to the visits. The tutor, Pierre Gilliard, noted that the children had been instructed by the Tsarina never to mention Rasputin's name. He himself saw Rasputin only once, in an anteroom of the Palace, as he was preparing to leave. He recalled: 'I had the distinct impression I was in the presence of a sinister and evil being.' Mossolov seconded Gilliard's view, making reference to 'Rasputin the Sinister'.

The servants who spotted Rasputin at the Palace were equally disparaging. As early as the winter of 1908, a maid, Sophia Tyutcheva, was disconcerted to see a 'peasant in tight-fitting coat' in the darkened corridors. In the spring of 1910, Tyutcheva reported, with dismay, that Rasputin was visiting the Grand Duchesses at bedtime, when the girls were in their nightclothes.

The stolid Mossolov thought well of Tyutcheva, regarding her as a good influence on the sometimes unruly Imperial children: 'Their manners at once showed great improvement.' He set store by her sense of propriety and now reported her views with approval: 'Tyutcheva's opinion was that the unsavoury *muzhik* [peasant] should not be allowed at night among the children.' But when Tyutcheva complained to the Tsar, she found him unreceptive, replying dramatically: 'I am alive only thanks to his prayers.' Tyutcheva was duly fired.

Another maid from the Court, Maria Vishnyakova, had an altogether more serious complaint. She claimed she had been assaulted and raped during a visit to Pokrovskoye. She said that Rasputin had 'started kissing me. I was in hysterics, he took my virginity'. When she complained, the Tsarina dismissed her testimony, insisting that everything about Rasputin was holy. The impasse was broken only when Vishnyakova lost her credibility after being found in bed with a cossack. She, too, was sacked.

Rasputin at the Alexandra Palace with the Tsarina, the maid Maria Vishnyakova and all five Imperial children

With relations at Court growing thornier, Rasputin also found himself losing supporters in the Church. First among these was his former houseguest and fishing companion, the monk Iliodor, who was becoming increasingly deranged, locking himself in a monastery at Tsaritzyn with thousands of his followers. At the end of his services he would decapitate a makeshift dragon he called Revolution. He built tunnels under the monastery and, in a final act of hubris, planned to build a massive tower.

Unleashing attacks upon his old friend, Iliodor complained that Rasputin 'emitted a disagreeable odour' and was bad with old ladies. He quoted Rasputin dismissing one elderly petitioner: 'Your love pleases me, mother, but God ain't with it.' He insisted the Synod take steps against Rasputin, or he would renounce his faith. The Synod responded, instead, by ordering him to leave Tsaritzyn and join another, distant monastery.

Unaware of the extent of Iliodor's betrayal, Rasputin was initially protective of him. He spoke up on his behalf when the Tsar also tried to order him to leave Tsaritzyn. He told the Tsar that, if he did not stop persecuting Iliodor, God would take revenge on the sickly Tsarevich. But later, on learning the truth, he switched sides without hesitation, barking: 'File his teeth.'

The Tsar decided to send a loyal aide de camp, Alexander Mandryka, to Tsaritzyn to deal with Iliodor. But

Above: Rasputin with Hermogen and Iliodor
Below: With his followers at Gorokhovaya Street

Mandryka ended up being distracted by shocking tales of Rasputin's debauchery. The nuns at Tsaritzyn were claiming that, during his visit, Rasputin had been conducting orgies and bathing with novices. When Mandryka returned and met the Tsar, on February 10 1911, his reports on Iliodor were eclipsed by these shocking stories: 'It is even said he [Rasputin] enjoyed the favour of Her Majesty,' Mandryka concluded, before bursting into tears. The Tsar felt obliged to send for a glass of water.

So Iliodor's rabble-rousing continued, for the moment, unchecked. But his *coup de grâce*, in terms of mischief-making, came in late 1911 when he copied and disseminated the letters he had pocketed at Pokrovskoye. None of his sermons could have unleashed the mayhem created by these innocent outpourings from the four young Grand Duchesses and their mother, the Tsarina, to their Man of God.

The letters from the girls were almost theatrically fond. Grand Duchess Olga wrote: 'It is hard without you, there is no one to tell my troubles to.' Her younger sister, Tatiana, asked: 'How's Matriosha [Maria]. Whenever we get together at Anya's [Anna Vyrubova's] we always talk about all of you, we miss you, we miss you... Mother is ill without you.' It was Tatiana who recorded conversations with Rasputin and kept all his letters to the family.

Grand Duchess Maria, the third daughter, who slept with a Bible given to her by Rasputin, wrote: 'I am kissing you. Kissing your pure hands... Let me see you alone about God.' The youngest, Grand Duchess Anastasia, then aged ten echoed: 'I kiss you and bless me.'

The Tsarina's letter, unfortunately, seemed to go beyond fondness: 'I wish to fall asleep on your shoulder. I love you. I believe in you. I kiss you warmly'. The words were misleading; she was not in love but in the throes of a sort of religious hysteria. There was no impropriety intended; these declarations came from a woman of such modesty that she assiduously covered the lavatory and bath when they were not in use.

One of the braver ministers took the Tsarina's letter to the Tsar, who glanced at it and shoved it in a drawer, commenting drily: 'Yes the letter is genuine.' He fired the Minister, A. A. Makarov, a few days later.

It was a rough period for Rasputin. And there was to be no let-up. The Tsar had barely recovered from Mandryka's outburst and Iliodor's public exposure of the Tsarina's passionate letter before Rasputin arrived at the Palace bearing compromising photographs of himself cavorting with a Finnish ballerina. He had fallen victim to what would become a common Soviet tactic: discrediting by way of 'kompromat'. He had been told that unless he left St Petersburg the photographs would be shown to the Tsar, and so he had opted for a pre-emptive strike.

His tactic paid off, with the Tsar declaring simply that Rasputin had been weak and allowed himself to be exploited by revolutionaries. The Tsarina was probably never told about the photographs.

asputin managed to brush off these slings and arrows, not least Iliodor's rages against him. He would have a harder time dealing with the rancour of the more senior members of the Church. By the beginning of 1910, the most fervent of his early supporters, Bishop Feofan, was having insurmountable doubts about his Man of God. His earlier worries about the lavish furnishings at Pokrovskoye had been overshadowed by complaints of Rasputin abusing and even raping women. He wrote an anguished letter to another highly regarded priest, Hermogen, who had also once supported Rasputin, convinced that 'the devout fire flowed in his soul'.

Hermogen, a former lawyer, was very conservative and had no truck with the Duma, the recently established Russian parliament, which he denounced as an 'enemy of Orthodox Russian people'. He had a high-pitched voice and it was rumoured that he had castrated himself in a religious fervour. Feofan informed Hermogen that Rasputin was in a state of 'spiritual temptation' and that he 'didn't occupy the highest level of spiritual life'.

It turned out Hermogen had also changed his mind about the Man of God after catching him trying to seduce the wife of another priest. More crucially, having read Iliodor's letters, he believed that Rasputin was sleeping with the Tsarina. Hermogen demanded immediate action, suggesting kidnapping Rasputin and searching his flat.

Feofan favoured the less dramatic option of complaining to the Tsarina, but she was dismissive, insisting that stories of Rasputin's misdemeanours were all 'falsehood and slander'. She even suggested that Feofan was jealous of Brother Grigory. Feofan then wrote to the Tsar that he had heard a confession from a woman who had been seduced by Rasputin. He received no reply. The Bishop finally confronted Rasputin himself, ordering him to leave St Petersburg: 'Go away, you fraud.' Rasputin appeared repentant, weeping and begging forgiveness. But he had no intention of leaving and instead scurried straight to the Palace to complain to the Tsarina. The troublesome Bishop Feofan developed facial palsy, lung disease and malaria and was dispatched to the Crimea.

But Rasputin hadn't quite finished with him. The Provisional Government's Commission was told that, in October 1913, a stranger approached the wife of a paralysed priest, offering her 1,000 roubles if she would say that Feofan had told her the Tsarina was sleeping with Rasputin. The woman later received a letter in a fine hand, presumably not Rasputin's, telling her to think again and tell the truth.

The Tsarina fought back against Feofan and Hermogen, commissioning a study, 'Russian Saints Who Were Holy Fools in Christ', in which she underlined passages describing the Saints' 'sexual dissoluteness'. She ignored the fact that these particular holy fools in Christ were debauched only before their conversions, when they were young: Rasputin was by then a seasoned 40 years old. The author of the study was amply rewarded and later pronounced: 'I don't care about Rasputin. Thanks to him, I'm now a prelate making 18,000 roubles a year, with all the fringe benefits.'

*Rasputin's aphorisms included, on
marriage: 'A good graft revives an
old tree'; he would admonish the rich:
'You could feed five villages with what's
hanging on your walls.'*

What the churchmen made of Rasputin's next move is not known; but, at the Tsar's suggestion, he journeyed to the Holy Land. Upon his return, the Tsarina and Anna Vyrubova collaborated with him on a thin volume: 'My Thoughts and Meditations: A Short Description of Visits to the Holy Places'. Rasputin proudly presented his book to friends, inscribed with a large, shaky 'G'. In the opening passages he makes much of his joy at leaving St Petersburg, a centre of 'vain and worldly things', where 'we slumber and fall into evil ways'. Alongside his book about Jerusalem, Rasputin's works include 'Pious Meditations' and 'Life of an Experienced Wanderer'.

The Tsarina never tired of his ministrations. When she had a headache, she insisted: 'I write down the saying of our Friend and the time passes more quickly.' Rasputin's aphorisms included, on marriage: 'A good graft revives an old tree', and on a prospective trip: 'Before crossing the river, see that the ferry is in its place'. He would admonish the rich: 'You could feed five villages with what's hanging on your walls', and instruct city dwellers: 'Go out of the town into the fields' while insisting they do not pick flowers: 'It is cruel to take life by force.'

On national traits he proclaimed: 'The worst Russian has a better soul than foreigners.' Finally he made a strong pronouncement on women following a rebuff from a Muscovite: 'Peter women better than Moscow women.' This last proclamation was delivered to the accompaniment of smashing plates. The Tsarina was impressed by Rasputin's resourcefulness. She liked the way he always had a remedy up his sleeve, sometimes literally: he would create poultices by boiling water and mashing it up with crumbling pieces of oak bark picked from his grubby pockets.

But the Imperial couple's various strategies to cleanse Rasputin's reputation were never going to appease the clerics. Hermogen decided to summon Rasputin to his quarters at the Yaroslavl Monastery in December 1911. It is a mark of Rasputin's self-confidence that he suspected nothing of what was in store. In fact, he thought he was enjoying a rare break from hostilities. Within the previous few months, the turncoat Feofan had been seen off by the Tsarina. Meanwhile, his old enemy, Stolypin, had been shot in a theatre in Kiev, dying five days later. The Tsar had rushed to his hospital bedside, fallen to his knees and whispered ominously: 'Forgive me.'

It turned out that Rasputin had earlier spotted Stolypin in the street, and said: 'Death is stalking him.' But this was seen less as a prophecy than a reaction to Stolypin's sickly appearance. After her initial shock at the assassination, the Tsarina observed coldly: 'Those who have offended our Friend may no longer count on divine protection.' Striking the final blow, Rasputin produced a book describing the celebrations of 1911, during which Stolypin had been murdered. He called it 'Great Festivities in Kiev!'

So after Hermogen contacted him, Rasputin may even have been looking forward to a get-together with the clerics. He readily agreed to be collected by Iliodor, on December 16; coincidentally the same date as his fateful midnight assignation with Yussoupov five years later. He was clearly unaware, at that point, that Iliodor already loathed him.

He swept buoyantly out of his flat in a 2,000-rouble fur coat. But when he arrived at the monastery, he was immediately brought down to size by the dwarf 'Blessed Mitya' in ascetic's rags. Mitya pronounced – presumably through his interpreter – that Rasputin should be killed or castrated, adding: 'You have offended many nurses. You are sleeping with the Tsarina. You are an anti-Christ.' He then set about punching Rasputin, before grabbing his penis and trying to pull it off.

Rasputin tried to push Mitya away: he finally succeeded, sending the 'little prophet' flying across the room. But before he could straighten up, the stately Hermogen had begun beating him on the back with a heavy cross, accusing him of suffering from a sickness he called satyriasis.

Hermogen dragged Rasputin to the chapel and made him swear never to see the Tsar and Tsarina again, adding: 'Don't return to Russia for three years.' The fiery Iliodor, wielding an axe, now weighed in, agreeing with Mitya that Rasputin should be castrated. Iliodor wanted Rasputin sent to the prison island Sakhalin; the lavish house in Pokrovskoye must be burnt to the ground. Rasputin eventually managed to wrest himself free and shot out of the room, before locking the angry clerics in by propping a chair up under the doorknob.

As soon as he had recovered himself, Rasputin fired off complaints to both the Tsarina and the Synod. Retribution was swift: Hermogen was ordered into exile to the Jirovitsky Monastery in Vladimir Oblast, denied his rights to a hearing. When he wrote requesting an audience in order to divulge certain secrets, the Tsar replied that he didn't want to know them. Instead, he was bundled unceremoniously into a car and driven to the station. Iliodor was eventually chased to ground, arrested and sent to the Florishchev Monastery, where he set about plotting to kill Rasputin; such was his zeal that, at one point, he accrued 120 bombs.

Iliodor now denounced the Imperial couple, dismissing the Tsar, at five feet four inches, as 'a little man'. He himself was proud to resemble a Volga brigand, with hands the size of large stones. He added that the Tsar, a keen tippler and smoker, was a 'drunk weed puffer'. In fact, there were claims that Rasputin had cured the Tsar of his drinking habit, with an elaborate procedure involving complex switches of wines and glasses. He had also cured his friend Simanovich, who swore to the cure's efficacy: 'I never drank again for as long as I lived.' But Iliodor knew nothing of any cures. He carried on raging against the Imperial Family, finally insisting that the Tsarina was 'debauched' and that Alexis was fathered by Rasputin.

When the Synod failed to take action against Rasputin, Iliodor dismissed it as a 'House of Pigs' and signed a renunciation of faith in his own blood. Asked subsequently to give his religion at hotel reception desks, he declared himself Iliodorian.

hrough the early months of 1912, opposition to Rasputin continued to grow. The Speaker of the Duma, Alexander Guchkov, was known for resorting to fist fights during sessions, but he was uncharacteristically restrained in his first speech against Rasputin, referring to him discreetly as 'dark forces'. The Man of God was not fooled, writing a plaintive note: 'Dear Papa and Mama! Now the accursed demon gains strength. And the Duma serves him, there are a lot of revolutionaries and Yids in it... And Guchkov, their lord... slanders and makes a discord...'

On March 9, Guchkov made further discord with a more direct speech attacking Rasputin as 'an enigmatic tragicomic figure, a kind of ghost or relic of age-old ignorance.' He continued to rage: 'By what avenues has this man achieved his central position? By having seized such influence that even the supreme bearers of State and Church power bow down before it!... Just think who is lording it at the summit!' The Tsarina was furious, snapping back: 'Guchkov needs to be on a high tree.'

The Tsar's mother, once so anxious about the Court mystic M. Philippe, was consumed with worry about the increasingly public controversy surrounding Rasputin. She arranged to meet her son and daughter-in-law for an urgent discussion and emerged believing she had carried the day. The Tsar's sister, Grand Duchess Xenia, wrote in her diary: 'Mama is so pleased that she said everything... Alex [the Tsarina] defended Rasputin, saying he was a remarkable man and Mama should meet him... Mama merely advised them to let him go now... Alex declared that it was wrong to yield... But they were still very grateful to Mama for having spoken so frankly. And she even kissed Mama's hand.'

It is hard to gauge what affect, if any, the Dowager's words had upon the Imperial couple. It seems very unlikely that either was truly grateful for the Dowager's 'frankness'. The Tsar's diary entry is particularly non-committal: 'Mama came for tea; we had a conversation with her about Grigory.'

But shortly afterwards, the Tsar asked the fearsome Mikhail Rodzyanko, President of the Duma, to launch an investigation into Rasputin's life. In the course of several subsequent inquiries, Rodzyanko would hear of at least one woman petitioner instructed by Rasputin to return in a décolleté dress in order to secure her husband's promotion. As Rasputin would put it: 'All right, I'll see to it. But come again tomorrow in an open dress with naked shoulders. Otherwise don't bother.'

Rodzyanko was under no illusion about the sensitive nature of his final report. Before seeing the Tsar, he steeled himself with a prayer in the Kazan Cathedral. The Tsar's response to Rodzyanko's brave denunciation is not recorded in any detail. But when Rodzyanko raised the thorny issue of women in the bath-house, the Tsar retorted that communal bathing was 'accepted among the common people'. Rodzyanko seemed to make headway when he produced a picture of Rasputin dressed as a priest and the Tsar commented: 'This time he's gone too far.' But the principal outcome of the report was to drive a wedge between Rodzyanko and the Tsar. The Tsar eventually refused to see him and cut him dead at a service commemorating the Battle of Borodino in Moscow in 1912. As Rodzyanko explained grimly: 'His dissatisfation with me was my report on Rasputin.'

It was during this same year that the 24-year-old Englishman, Gerald Hamilton, the model for Isherwood's Mr Norris, paid Rasputin two visits. Hamilton saw nothing of any 'dark forces' and was, in fact, deeply impressed by Rasputin, particularly when he saw him performing a cure on a young epileptic boy. 'The boy was brought forward by his mother and sat in a chair. Rasputin first looked at him; then he put his hands on him, muttering prayers. Later the boy twitched a lot, but Rasputin never took his hands off his chest. This huge man became paler and paler until finally the boy... got up and ran to his mother. It took about seven minutes in all.'

After the cure, Hamilton recalled that Rasputin collapsed dramatically into a chair proclaiming: 'All the good has gone out of me, and I must get new strength. I have been fighting the evil spirits in that poor boy.' The story is slightly undermined by Hamilton's recollection that the cure took place at Gorokhovaya Street when, in fact, Rasputin did not move there until 1914.

Hamilton remained resolutely enamoured of Rasputin; he was not in the least put out when he heard that Rasputin did not care for the English: 'I considered it a great privilege to have seen undeniable proof of his extraordinary gift of healing. It may seem profane to mention Jesus Christ in any connection with Rasputin but for all I know God may choose odd vessels to do his work.'

As fresh attacks were launched in the Duma and at

Court, it may have struck Rasputin's beleaguered supporters that some vessels could be too odd.

But in October 1912 an event occurred which raised Rasputin's stock at the Palace and, for a while, rendered him unassailable. He was on one of his frequent visits to Pokrovskoye at the time: 'going for a little home', as the Tsarina put it blithely. The purpose of these endless returns was twofold: he appeased his detractors by keeping a low profile while gratifying his weakness for creature comforts and soft furnishings. He may even have welcomed a respite from the dizziness of his life in St Petersburg, with its unending array of colourful characters.

As he was walking along the River Tura with his daughter Maria, he suddenly clutched his head and told her something had happened to the Tsarevich Alexis: 'He's been stricken.' A couple of days later he received a telegram from Anna Vyrubova saying that Alexis was mortally ill in a hunting lodge at Spala, in Poland.

The Rasputins were in the middle of a family lunch when the telegram had arrived. Rasputin made one of his fierce gestures at the maid, Dounia, to stop doing dishes, while he left the room to pray. He was grey and sweating when he reappeared, but immediately set about composing a reply. He loved sending telegrams, not least because he could leave any awkward spellings to the telegraphist. He sent two messages: 'The Little

One will not die.... Do not let the doctors bother him too much.'

Alexis had injured his leg while jumping onto a boat. He seemed to have recovered, but the Tsarina had then taken him for a drive and the violent shaking of the carriage had brought on a stomach haemorrhage. His subsequent cries of pain were so heart-rending that the more sensitive servants resorted to ear-plugs. None of them would have known, at this point, that Alexis had haemophilia. His anxious doctors met regularly in Mossolov's room. As Mossolov recalled: 'None of the remedies which they prescribed sufficed to arrest the bleeding.'

The eight-year-old boy himself was prepared to die, instructing his despairing parents to bury him beneath a blue sky and build a monument. The Tsar reluctantly agreed to issue a news bulletin announcing that the Tsarevich was ill; bulletins were posted as far away as Siberia. A tent erected on the lodge lawn for worship was soon being visited by weeping Polish peasants. The fervent Father Vassiliev performed the last rites.

Alexis began to recover the day Rasputin's first telegram arrived from Pokrovskoye. The Tsarina was convinced that, without Rasputin's prayer, her son would have died. As she said to Mossolov: 'It's not the first time the *starets* [Holy Man] has saved his life.' The doctors were apparently confounded. One of them, Professor Federov, had at one point asked Mossolov's advice, asking whether he should risk experimenting without telling the Tsar or Tsarina. As Mossolov wrote: 'Professor Federov said: "Should I prescribe without

Above: Alexis after Spala
Below: The Imperial Family

saying anything?'" After the spectacular recovery, Mossolov asked Federov if he had applied some secret remedy; but Federov replied, tantalisingly, that even if he had, he couldn't have admitted it.

The Tsarevich's journey back to Russia was meticulously planned. The roads were smoothed between the hunting lodge and the station; the train to St Petersburg travelled at 15mph and never once used its brakes. Mossolov reported that the doctors at Spala were not consulted about the fragile Tsarevich's departure and were deeply upset to have found themselves so promptly sidelined. When the Tsar described the crisis to his mother, he made no mention of Rasputin's telegrams.

Relations between 'our Friend' and the Palace had never been closer. By the time the Imperial family reached St Petersburg, Rasputin and his two daughters had also returned. The Tsarina telephoned on arrival and Maria gushed: 'Mama, I have missed you.' The girl was ecstatic to receive a further call, from Anna Vyrubova, issuing a coy invitation for tea to meet 'a certain family'.

The Tsarina's view of the Russian aristocracy as decadent had been formed during her first days in the capital. Coming originally from the quieter German Court of Darmstadt, she had been shocked by the loose society, all-night parties and flaunted love affairs: 'The heads of the young ladies of St Petersburg are filled with nothing but thoughts of young officers,' she had sniffed.

Her misgivings resulted in the Imperial children's social lives being woefully restricted. Dr Botkin's son, Gleb, recalled that their only friends were the children of Alexis's sailor carer, Andrei Derevenko, and Rasputin's two daughters. The Grand Duchesses met the Misses Rasputin relatively late on, in 1912; but for Gleb, it was not late enough: he dismissed them as 'veritable street urchins'.

In fact, Maria, now 14, had already been in St Petersburg for two years and was quite accomplished: able to play tennis, accompany herself singing and hold forth about fashion. Born Matryona, she had adopted the smarter name of 'Maria': she might have been glad to distance herself from the ragged mystic, Matryona the Barefoot.

The Rasputin girls would have had a smattering of high culture from their father. The Man of God had developed an unlikely taste for opera and ballet; he was said to have enjoyed particularly a performance by Chaliapin in Mussorgsky's *Boris Godunov*. And both sisters were, of course, suitably religious, praying for hours under Rasputin's beady eye: such was their father's strictness that they regarded sitting on their heels while kneeling as a major transgression.

Nonetheless, Maria found her first tea at Anna Vyrubova's house a challenge. She successfully selected a dress with a sailor's collar, but admitted to being thrown, when, braced for a curtsey, she found herself swept up by the Tsarina for a kiss. She struggled to find a conversational gambit, finally hitting upon: 'You must have hundreds of servants.' The Tsarina agreed, putting Maria at her ease, but then added, less truthfully, that she could easily manage without them. Conversation between Maria and the young Grand Duchesses ran more smoothly, though the Tsarina would have disapproved of the topic: the Grand Duchesses enthused fancifully about the 'handsome officers' with whom they danced or played tennis.

The eldest, Olga, plied Maria with questions about her life, both in Pokrovskoye and St Petersburg. The Grand Duchesses thought the Rasputins exotic because they went to school. The Tsarina had tried to get Maria and her sister Varya into the glamorous Smolny Institute for young ladies but both girls had been rejected. They were now happily installed at a regular *Gymnasium*. The Grand Duchesses were lost in admiration when they heard that the racy sisters enjoyed a weekly visit to the cinema.

Maria maintained that the Tsarina was sufficiently taken with her to issue a separate invitation for dinner. Over prawns, herring and caviar, the Tsarina informed Maria that she must put her cutlery on a rack while she was eating. If she left knives or forks on her plate, it would be assumed that she had finished. The dinner was apparently rounded off with a rich dessert incorporating ten egg yolks and a quart of cream, called ice cream Romanov. After dinner, the Tsarina insisted that she loved Maria and wanted her to live at the Palace. The girl sat at the Tsarina's knee on a silken pillow.

On November 29, Rasputin received another clean bill of health from the Church. The endorsement had a slightly dodgy provenance, coming as it did from Bishop Alexis of Tobolsk, a known protector of the *khlysty*. Howeve, this would not have bothered Rasputin. Bishop Alexis had been happy to issue the endorsement and happier still to accept, as a reward, his promotion to Exarch of Georgia.

The year 1913 marked the 300th year of Romanov rule. It also saw Rasputin over-reaching himself, becoming embroiled in ever more scrapes as he hogged prime spots during the grand celebrations.

At the Kazan Cathedral, in February, he stationed himself in a seat reserved for members of the Duma. The Duma President Rodzyanko grew livid when, amid the finery, he spotted Rasputin in a sort of fancy dress: 'He was luxuriously clad in a dark-raspberry silk peasant shirt, high patent leather boots, wide black trousers and a black peasant's shirt.' Rodzyanko ordered him to move, but the Man of God sat tight and glared at him. Rodzyanko then grabbed him by the scruff of the neck and, as Rasputin fell theatrically to his knees, kicked him in the ribs. Rasputin was removed by guards, tut-tutting: 'Lord forgive him such sin.' Rasputin's temerity here is to be admired: Rodzyanko once described himself to the Tsarevich as the 'largest, fattest man in Russia'. It was said that, on a clear day, his voice could be heard a full kilometre away.

At another celebration, at Kostroma, in May, Rasputin again took a prominent seat next to the altar and refused to move. This time he managed to stay put, even though he technically had no right to be there at all: Vladimir Dzunkovsky, the former Governor of Moscow, had made a point of refusing his request for a ticket. The Tsar's sister, Grand Duchess Xenia, was horrified at witnessing the resulting 'displeasure and protest among the clergymen'. At the Kremlin, Rasputin created a stir again, grabbing yet another coveted seat. Xenia noted in her diary that 'Rasputin was all over the place... How will it all end?'

She was smartly rebuffed when she expressed her worries to the Tsarina: 'Of Grigory she said how could she not believe in him, when she saw how "The Little One" got better whenever he [Rasputin] was near him or praying for him.' Felix Yussoupov's mother went to the Palace to complain about Rasputin, at the behest of the Tsarina's own sister Ella, but was given short shrift: 'I hope we never meet again,' snapped the Tsarina.

From this point on there would be a split within the Romanovs. The Tsar's immediate family supported Rasputin, while every other member opposed him. The Tsar's mother, the Dowager, was bitterly disappointed that nothing had come of her 'frank' tea with her son and daughter-in-law: the 'holy fool Grishka' was still at Court: 'She [her daughter-in-law] is bringing about her own downfall and that of the dynasty... She deeply believes in that dubious individual.' She lamented to Rodzyanko: 'My son is too pure of heart to believe in evil.' In the end the Dowager gave her son a clear choice: if he would not send Rasputin away from St Petersburg, she herself would leave. She was the one who left, to live in Kiev.

But the Imperial couple's faith in 'our Friend' was not to be shaken. On July 16, the Tsar wrote in his diary that Alexis's 'right elbow began to hurt from waving his arms about too much while playing. He could not sleep for a long time and was in great pain, poor thing!' Rasputin came the next day: 'Soon after his departure the pain in Alexis's arm started to disappear, he became calmer and began to fall asleep.'

At the beginning of 1914, there was jubilation among Rasputin's supporters when one of our Friend's friends was appointed Prime Minister. The 75-year-old Ivan Goremykin had moustaches to his shoulders, fell asleep during meetings and jauntily referred to himself as 'a man of the old school' and an 'old coat'. Yussoupov's mother called him, more elaborately, 'a fur coat in moth balls'. But Rasputin insisted that the elderly Goremykin understood one of life's most important messages, that 'one need not be shaken by the changing waves'.

Goremykin replaced Vladimir Kokovstov, who had fallen from favour after an unfortunate tea with Rasputin. Kokovstov's initial dismay over Rasputin's table manners had given way to rage as he became convinced he was being hypnotised: 'When tea was served, Rasputin seized a handful of biscuits, threw them into his tea and again fixed his lynx-like eyes on me.' Kokovstov had appealed to the Tsar's mother: 'She wept bitterly and promised to speak to Nicholas. But she had little hope of success.' Kokovstov had been, in any case, a marked man since labelling 'our Friend' a 'Siberian tramp'.

Rasputin and the new Prime Minister were as thick as thieves. The unlikely friendship forged between the two men marked Rasputin's first real dabble in mainstream politics and gave rise to increasing consternation among his critics. Rasputin sent Goremykin streams of respectfully worded petitions: 'Dear Elder of God, listen to them, assist them, if you can, with apologies, Grigory'; 'Dear friend, be so kind do it for me.' He would prepare piles of scribbled notes in advance and at some pains; as he was fond of saying: 'I don't even know the alphabet.' On Goremykin's birthday, Rasputin sent boxes of cigars and pheasants. He gave Goremykin's wife cures over the telephone and she returned the compliment by delivering hot meals to his flat: she knew ten different ways to cook potatoes.

During the early months of 1914, Rasputin enjoyed a period of relative calm. However many Romanovs were ranged against him, he enjoyed the support of the Tsar, the Tsarina and the Prime Minister of all the Russias.

He moved to Gorokhovaya Street with his daughters Maria and Varya in May. The street was known for being down at heel. The impoverished anti-hero of Dostoyevsky's *Crime and Punishment* is often named as its most famous previous resident; in fact Raskolnikov's squalid rooms were probably two streets away. But Gorokhovaya Street was situated yards from the station for trains to Tsarskoye Selo, where the Imperial family were spending most of their time. Within minutes of a phone summons, 'our Friend' could be well on his way to the Alexander Palace.

A curious article published that summer boosted Rasputin's reputation for extrasensory perception. The writer wanted to test his actually rather shaky 'gift for knowing people'. He showed him a portrait of Karl Marx and recorded his reaction. Rasputin became over-excited, switching on an electric light and examining Marx's features closely: 'He's a Samson, my friend, a real Samson, yes, sir! Introduce me to him! We'll go to see him right now! That's somebody the people should follow in regiments!' Though the test results were presented in a positive light, Rasputin's comments were quite vague and he seemed to miss the crucial detail: that Marx had been dead more than 30 years.

Such was Rasputin's mood, at this point, that he was not in the least put out when the Tsar suggested that, despite the ostensible calm, he should return again to Pokrovskoye for a 'bit of home'. He would have been consoled by 75,000 roubles from the Tsarina, smartly followed by a fond telegram dated April 9: 'Pokrovskoye from Tsarskoye Selo for Novy. I am with you with all my heart, all my thoughts. Pray for me and Nicholas on the bright day [the anniversary of their engagement]. Love and kisses – Darling.'

According to some reports the Tsar had, in fact, been intending to banish Rasputin to Pokrovskyoe for good; for all her reputation for stinginess, the Tsarina was proffering him a generous farewell gift. As it turned out, the irrepressible Man of God would return to St Petersburg within months.

But it was while Rasputin was back in Pokrovskoye at the end of June that he suffered the first serious attempt on his life. He had been standing at the gate of his house, puzzling over a telegram from the Tsarina telling him that Alexis had twisted his ankle, when an ill-favoured woman asked him for money. As he groped about in his pockets for a modest five-kopeck piece, the woman stabbed him in the chest. 'And I could feel blood pouring from me,' he recalled.

His first reaction was to hit his assailant on the shoulder, but he then found himself defending her as she was set upon by a lynch mob of his supporters. Maria remembered the crowd shouting: 'Kill her, we'll drown her in the Tura.' His proud boast at the time was 'Grishka stood up for her.' But he soon reverted to hostility, referring to her as 'the slut who stuck a knife up my arse.'

His attacker, Khiona Guseva, was aged 33 and had no nose. Rasputin and his son, Dmitri, had noticed her at mass the preceding Sunday and Rasputin had reprimanded his son for pointing out how odd she looked. It was rumoured that, at 13, she had suffered a bad reaction to medicine and that her nose had become severely infected. There was another story that her nose had been lost, in adulthood, to syphilis.

Whatever happened, she could not, like Gogol's hero of 'The Nose', simply have woken up without one. Gogol's hero addressed the shame of being noseless after tracking down a giant-size version of his nose, praying in the Kazan Cathedral: 'You will agree that it's not done for someone in my position to walk around minus a nose. It's all right for some old woman selling peeled oranges on the Voskresensky Bridge...'

But Rasputin was not interested in any poignant details: 'If I had been stabbed by a beauty... But that noseless stinker!' he would rant. The Pokrovskoye police description of Guseva was stark: 'nose absent, irregular hole in place'.

He would have been horrified to hear subsequent rumours that Guseva was his former lover. But then it was said that she had once been a milliner and nick-named 'little princess' because of her elegant bearing and intellectual finesse. The truth was that she now lived in Tsaritzyn, home town of Rasputin's staunchest current enemy, Iliodor. She was a devoted follower of Iliodor, who was convinced that she had lost her nose after nobly asking God to take away her beauty.

At the beginning of that summer, Iliodor is said to have strung a knife around Guseva's neck and ordered her to kill Rasputin. She had dutifully stalked her victim from Yalta to St Petersburg and finally to Pokrovskoye. There she had rented a room and kept watch over the lavish Rasputin house from a window. During the day, she had stationed herself strategically on a particular wooden bench. At her subsequent trial Guseva was in-vited to plead insanity or 'religious ecstasy'. She refused, insisting she was sane, but still ended up, a mad hatter, in the Tomsk Regional Clinic for the Insane.

After the stabbing, Rasputin was carried into his house. His devoted wife Praskovia sent plates crash-ing to the floor as she cleared the dining table. He was laid out and operated on by a doctor using just the light from a candle. Maria wrote proudly that her father re-fused any anaesthetic. A priest was called to hear his last confession and, according to Maria, the Rasputins' lachrymose icon of the Virgin of Kazan wept again: a servant who was dusting the Virgin's face spotted drops of water. Rasputin sent a lurid telegram to the Tsarina: 'That hunk of carrion struck me with a knife.' Her reply was equally passionate: 'Our grief is beyond description, we hope for God's goodness.'

He had to be taken in a carriage to Tyumen for another operation. According to Maria, well-wishers gathered outside the house: 'Peasants weeping and lamenting escorted the stretcher.' Along the way, Maria and Dounia cushioned Rasputin's body against Trakt 4's infamous bumps.

When they reached the hospital, Rasputin was robust enough to insist that he wanted no journalists within cannon shot. But one canny reporter, from the *Stock Exchange News*, managed to inveigle his way into Rasputin's ward, reporting: 'He sat worn out by ill health in a hospital smock.' The doctor who operated on Rasputin received a gold watch from his grateful patient and orders were issued to female carers 'not to wear corsets'. There was clearly life in the old dog. Among visitors during his 46-day stay, bringing gifts from the faithful, was his most voluptuous 'little lady', Akilina Laptinskaya.

In August 1914, while Rasputin was still at State Hospital 649, war was declared. Rasputin was much upset, tearing his bandages and shouting: 'Let Papa and Mama not plan war.' He insisted he'd had a dream in which he saw the 'Neva [river] full of the blood of Grand Dukes'. He apparently wrote with curious lucidity to the Tsar: 'You are the Tsar, the father of your people. Don't let the lunatics triumph and destroy you and the people. And if we conquer Germany, what, in truth, will happen to Russia? We all drown in blood: the disaster is great; the misery infinite.' He dispatched a more characteristic telegram to the Palace, which was unfortunately leaked to the Duma: 'Don't declare war. Fire Nikolasha [Grand Duke Nicholas].'

Rasputin had turned against Grand Duke Nicholas. He was no longer grateful for his generosity regarding Praskovia's hysterectomy and made no secret of his new-found disapproval of the Grand Duke's marriage to the Black Princess Anastasia. The Grand Duke had, in his turn, lost faith in the dog-healing Man of God. He had been shocked by Rasputin's attacks on saints and churchmen, dismayed by his opposition to the war and mortified to hear of attacks upon himself. But at this early stage, the Tsar was in agreement with Grand Duke Nicholas, making one of his few, short-lived stands against Rasputin: 'Our domestic affairs are not subject to the influence of others.'

During his recuperation, Rasputin visited another of his controversial cleric friends, Bishop Varnava, in Tobolsk. Rasputin had been behind Varnava's unpopular promotion to Bishop. The Bishop, in turn, had proved his own loyalty to Rasputin by joining the voluptuous 'little lady' Laptinskaya at his hospital bedside. Varnava's eccentric tastes included a predilection for having photographs taken of himself in coffins. The Tsarina, however, found him decidedly unphotogenic, comparing him to a 'rodent with bushy tail and fat body'.

On his journey back to Pokrovskoye, Rasputin decided to protect himself from further attacks by dressing up in a white dress and bonnet. Coincidentally, at almost the same moment, the murderous Iliodor was fleeing across the Russian border, also dressed as a woman.

When Rasputin returned to St Petersburg, he found it much changed. The city had been renamed the more Russian 'Petrograd'. As the troops were mobilised, a wave of patriotism had swept throughout Russia, with daily demonstrations held to support the Tsar. 'For Faith, Tsar and Country' and 'For the Defence of Holy Russia' were the rallying calls from factories and villages.

Upon his arrival at the flat, Rasputin phoned Anna Vyrubova and asked to see the Tsarina. Told he must wait a couple of days, he banged down the phone in annoyance. The 'Tsars' were reluctant to meet him because they knew of his opposition to the war. When they were all finally reunited, at Anna Vyrubova's house, Rasputin wept, while predicting more tears and blood: 'Dear friend, I will say again, a menacing cloud is over Russia... Lots of sorrow and grief, it is dark and there is no lightening to be seen.' The Tsarina made no reply, while the Tsar continued sipping his tea.

In the end Rasputin accepted that his opposition to the war would cost him vital support at Court. He performed one of his adroit about-turns and was soon confiding in the French Ambassador: 'I am always telling the Tsar that he must fight until complete victory is won,' adding hastily: 'I'm also telling him that war has brought unbearable suffering to the Russian people.'

However, he was not going to drop his stand against Grand Duke Nicholas. As the Tsarina wrote to her husband: 'Grigory loves you jealously and can't bear N taking a part.' Grand Duke Nicholas, in turn, roundly vetoed Rasputin's suggestion that he visit the battlefront: 'Come and I'll hang you.'

The Tsarina soon found Rasputin indispensable as a war-time helpmeet, particularly valuing his endorsement of her gruelling hospital visits. She wrote giddily to her husband: '27 Oct. 1914, We are going to another hospital now directly... We shall go as sisters (our Friend likes us to) & tomorrow also.' '21 November: this is the wire I just received from our Friend: "When you comfort the wounded God makes His name famous through your gentleness and glorious work". So touching & must give me strength to get over my shyness.' '28 November... At times I feel I can't any more & fill myself with heart-drops & it goes again – & our Friend wishes me beside to go.'

Rasputin himself would not have been so welcome. Many at the Imperial Court were put out by his burgeoning interest in the war wounded. Dr Botkin's son, Gleb, imagined the shocked reaction of soldiers on the steps of a military hospital, upon hearing the words of the Palace Commandant: 'The carriage for Mr Rasputin.'

That autumn the Man of God was himself fighting battles on various fronts. Aside from dealing with a growing band of enemies, he was plagued by worries that his powers were failing. In the previous year he had, according to the secret police, been reduced to brushing up his techniques as a hypnotist. The Okhrana had found a letter from Rasputin asking for lessons in hypnosis. A surveillance agent reported that the teacher of hypnotism had a moustache and was 'swarthy of face'.

Neither of 'the Tsars', needless to say, had any inkling of Rasputin's self-doubt. Shortly after their emotional tea, the Tsarina summoned him back to the Palace to help Alexis and pray by the boy's bedside. The Tsarina wrote to the Tsar: '19 September... You, I know, notwithstanding all you will have to do, will still miss yr little family & precious agoo wee one [Alexis]. He will quickly get better now that our Friend has seen him & that will be a great relief to you.'

The Tsarina met Rasputin regularly at Anna Vyrubova's house during this period. But, for all her confidence in 'our Friend', she was still worried about being seen with him: '23 Sept... Ania [as she called Anna] was offended I did not go to her, but she had lots of guests, & our Friend for three hours.' The following day they did meet. She wrote to the Tsar: '24 Sept... flew for half an hour... to Ania's house, as our Friend spent the afternoon with her & wanted to see me. He asked after you... may God give you courage, strength & patience – faith you have more than ever and it is this wh. keeps you up... And our Friend helps you carry yr. heavy cross and great responsibilities.'

Such was her faith in Rasputin as strategist that she was soon suggesting that she herself make contact with Nicholas Maklakov, the Minister of the Interior: '25 October... Our Friend came for an hour in the evening; he will await yr return and then go off for a little home... our Friend wishes me quickly to speak to Maklakov as he says one must not waste time until your return.'

When the Tsar returned to the Palace, he too gleaned support from Rasputin, writing at the end of October: 'Felt utter fury against the Germans and Turks for their foul attack in the Black Sea! Only in the evening, under the influence of Grigory's soothing words, did my soul regain its equilibrium.'

But the stabbing in Pokrovskoye had, according to several accounts, added five years to Rasputin's age. He began taking opium frequently and an old friend, who saw him at the time, said: 'He walked around hunched over in a gown.' Rasputin was shaken when he found himself unable to heal an old woman: 'The Lord has taken my power away from me.'

It was not until his dramatic cure of his stalwart Anna Vyrubova that he felt his vitality returning. He was with Mossolov, Director of the Imperial Court, when he heard that Anna had been seriously injured in an accident. Mossolov had been trying to gain Rasputin's support for a local government project and had already undergone one unproductive meeting: 'I waited half an hour. At last he appeared, his face bloated, his hair unkempt.' Following three bottles of wine, Mossolov appeared to carry the day as Rasputin said: 'As for me, what can I do but give the idea my blessing.'

'Russia's Ruling House' caricature by N. Ivanov.
Cartoons were published of the Tsarina cavorting
with Rasputin; schoolchildren sang lewd songs.

Mossolov felt, understandably, that the drunken meeting had been inconclusive and arranged to see Rasputin again, for dinner, in the house of a mutual friend. But this second discussion also went awry when, just as Rasputin was licking the soup off his fingers, he received one of his urgent phone calls. Was it his fascination with gadgetry, an over-blown sense of his own importance or some vision of the future that made Rasputin behave, in early 1915, as though he already owned a mobile phone? Wherever he went, he left numbers: he could always be reached.

On this occasion, he returned to the table white-faced and trembling: Anna, 'Annushka', had been in a train crash while travelling from Tsarskoye Selo to Petrograd. The train had come off the tracks in a heavy snowfall. He left for Tsarskoye Selo immediately, using a car belonging to another eminent supporter, Countess Witte, wife of the former Prime Minister. Upon his arrival, he discovered that Anna Vyrubova's colossal legs had been irreparably crushed. He prayed for her before giving one of his bald but accurate pronouncements: 'She will recover but she will always be a cripple.' After praying he collapsed, as was his wont, but was furious to find himself ignored by 'the Tsars' and left to crawl back to Gorokhovaya Street under his own steam. He complained bitterly to Dounia.

Hours after his return, however, the Tsarina telephoned, full of gratitude. She sent flowers and 'a basket of fruit so heavy that it had to be carried by two people'. Rasputin was delighted to find himself so much in favour again. But, as always, it seemed that any increase in his popularity at Court was accompanied by a stepping up of hostilities beyond. Four days after his healing session with Anna Vyrubova, he was nearly run over by a sledge driven by ill-wishers from Tsaritzyn.

Later that year, a young man, Simoniko Pahekadze, announced that he wanted to marry the 17-year old Maria, who now boasted 'enormous bright-coloured lips' and a flirtatious manner. 'She would pass the tip of her tongue over her broad, bright red lips in a kind of predatory animal movement,' reported a fascinated visitor. But shortly after the couple's engagement, it emerged that Pahekadze was among Rasputin's enemies and primarily interested in killing his prospective father-in-law. He drew a gun on Rasputin but then, apparently finding his fingers frozen on the trigger, ended up firing into his own chest. He survived and was thenceforth banished from Petrograd.

In the last two years of his life, Rasputin found his wobbly 'gift for knowing people' taxed to the limit as murderous enemies vied with the favour-seekers and devotees for his attention. Despite his poor grasp of figures, he was now being courted by industrialists asking him to act as a business consultant. He developed a rudimentary taste for investments, toying with starting his own newspaper ('they write such horrors about me') and putting money into a newly emerging cinema with sound. Some of his actual, less ambitious enterprises included various forms of mild extortion. He would charge, for instance, 2,000 roubles (roughly £200) for keeping a soldier from the front. In a one-off deal, he agreed to spring 400 Baptists from prison for refusing military service, for 1,000 roubles each. He demanded 250 roubles from a convicted forger for his release from prison. How much success he had with these ventures cannot be known exactly. And inevitably there were deals that went awry. An elderly baroness claimed Rasputin had swindled her out of 270,000 roubles after summoning Jesus in a seance: the case was not pursued, although an early investigation unearthed the florist who supplied a crown of thorns.

He was not short of income. On top of the government allowance of 10,000 roubles that he received each month, the syphilitic Protopopov paid him 1,000 roubles a month from his own pocket, for which doubtless he had his own mysterious political motivations.

Such was Rasputin's prestige that, in January 1915, he was visited by Countess Witte, seeking promotion for her grandson. 'The Countess Witte visited the Dark One on 8 and 25 January, both times wearing a thick veil,' reported a security branch agent. 'On 25 January she asked the doorman to escort her by the back stairway and gave him a three-rouble tip.'

It was in his role as businessman that Rasputin became embroiled in one of his worst scrapes. In March 1915 he arranged to meet prospective 'clients' at the Yar restaurant in Moscow. The meeting deteriorated when he began boasting that the Tsarina had sewn shirts for him. His bragging increased with drink, until he was roaring that 'the old girl' had slept with him. Asked if he really was Rasputin, he dropped his trousers and waved his penis. With his penis exposed, he carried on chatting with several female singers, while distributing notes saying: 'Love unselfishly.'

The eminent British diplomat, Robert Bruce Lockhart, who was attending an event at the Yar, later wrote in dismay: 'As we watched the music hall performance in the main hall, there was a violent fracas in one of the private rooms. Wild shrieks of a woman, a man's curses, broken glass and the banging of doors. Head-waiters rushed upstairs. The manager sent for the police... But the row and roaring continued... The cause of the disturbance was Rasputin – drunk and lecherous, and neither police nor management dared evict him.'

The police eventually took Rasputin away at 2.00am. The following day he left Moscow in disgrace, doubtless consoled by a crowd of 'little ladies' who gathered at the station to see him off. The business project under discussion at the Yar, it emerged, would have been lucrative for Rasputin, but sadly fell through; it concerned outsize underwear for the military.

The Assistant Minister of the Interior and Director of the Police, Vladimir Dzunkovsky, had already crossed swords with Rasputin. Now, following three months of inquiries into the incident, he handed a graphic report to the Tsar, who, somewhat at a loss, instructed Dzunkovsky to keep the report to himself. 'The sovereign... listened very attentively, but did not utter a single word during my report,' recalled the Assistant Minister. 'Then he extended his hand and asked: "Is it written out?" I removed the memorandum from the folder, the sovereign took it, opened his desk and put the memorandum inside.' Disobeying the Tsar, Dzunkovsky promptly showed a second copy of the report to Grand Duke Nicholas and also to Prince Yussoupov's future fellow conspirator, Grand Duke Dmitri. For this he was fired.

Rasputin was jubilant; as he had already told one of his policemen: 'Your Dzunkovsky's finished.' But the young Grand Duchesses would have been disappointed to see him go: they were great fans of his repertoire of bird calls.

The Tsarina's angry response was especially incoherent; it is hard to tell whether she was more exasperated with Dzunkovsky or her husband. 'He acts as a traitor and not as a devoted subject who ought to stand up for the Friends of his Sovereign,' she wrote to the Tsar. 'You see how he turns your words & orders round – the slanderers were to be punished... ah, it's so vile... If we let our Friend be persecuted we & our country shall suffer for it. Ah my love, when at last will you thump with her (sic) hand upon the table & scream at Dzunkovsky & others when they act wrongly – one does not fear you – they must be frightened of you.'

When Rasputin eventually saw the Tsar, he successfully defended himself with his usual pleas: it was hard for those seeking the path of truth and righteousness; he was a 'sinful man' but he couldn't help it. 'Despite my terrible sins, I am a Christ in miniature.'

Nikolai Sablin, the Commander of the Imperial yacht, the *Standart*, carried out a further investigation. He admitted later that he had been reluctant to mention the incident at the Yar to the Tsarina as it had had a 'morbid effect on her'. Sablin himself found tales of Rasputin's debauchery hard to believe, particularly when they involved women in elevated circles: 'It seemed impossible that any society woman, unless possibly a psychopath, could give herself to such a slovenly peasant.'

Rasputin's supporters found various defences for his worsening behaviour. The Tsarina came to believe that an imposter was posing as Rasputin and misbehaving in clubs. Others insisted any deterioration was linked to mental and physical trauma resulting from his stabbing in Pokrovskoye. As for Rasputin himself, he always had a homily to hand: 'It is wrong to pretend they [human desires] do not exist and to allow them through neglect to atrophy.' Of saints he would add that they 'turn to filth in order that, amid the filth, their aureole may shine with double brightness'.

Rasputin was becoming ever more brazen in his attitude to women. He took the adage 'faint heart never won fair maiden' a stage further, making aggressive passes at any woman not classifiable as 'elderly'. 'Is there something on your conscience that you haven't dared tell your confessor?' he would say to women. He would allude to the sex lives of horses before making his moves: 'Come, my lovely mare.' His female visitors were expected to feel blessed as he distributed boiled eggs in his soiled hands or gave them lumps of black bread dripping with soup. After enjoying his favourite fish stew, he would generously proffer a finger: 'Lick it clean.'

Confusing his prey, he would somehow succeed in occupying the moral high ground: his lust for a woman would be a measure of her impurity. He must have judged one princess, upon whom he advanced without preliminaries, as exceedingly impure: 'You are a tasty dish,' he cajoled her, fondling her breasts and sticking his fingers inside her collar. 'You know where the spirit is?' he asked her, before lifting the hem of her dress. 'It's here.' He owned a sofa so overused that its back had given way. Though he himself had been leaning on it when it broke, he always blamed one particular large woman: 'It's all the sister from Simbirsk.... It's goblinery.'

And yet Rasputin always took a protective stance when it came to the women close to him. On one occasion, he took the Tsarina's confidante, Lili Dehn, to task after seeing her out walking with a strange man who was, in fact, her own father. And his daughters were well supervised: suitors were allowed only half an hour to discuss fashion before being unceremoniously thrown out. These lofty attitudes he combined with finely honed advances upon married women: 'You have sad eyes. He torments you a lot.'

He considered fellow travellers on the long train journey from Petrograd to Pokrovskoye fair game. He liked trains, saying: 'Without railroads a peasant has to stay home because he can't walk all through Siberia.' This statement was, of course, untrue: he had once chosen to cover hundreds of miles on foot rather than stay home.

His female visitors were expected to feel blessed as he distributed boiled eggs in his soiled hands or gave them lumps of black bread dripping with soup. After enjoying his favourite fish stew, he would generously proffer a finger: 'Lick it clean.'

One of the best advantages of train journeys, for Rasputin, was the endless opportunities they offered for 'rejoicing'. There was a Madame S. whom he tried to seduce in his carriage, backing off only when she pulled his beard. Another female traveller was spotted in his compartment 'lying with the elder in her undergarments'.

He could not excuse his behaviour with pleas of deprivation. Although he hadn't had sexual relations with his wife since her hysterectomy, his Siberian maid Dounia, smitten since the age of 14, had been more than happy to move to Petrograd and step into Praskovia's shoes. According to Maria, their relationship had begun after he made a sudden lunge at her as she undressed him, provocatively, in her nightgown.

Prominent among his 'little ladies' at Gorokhovaya Street was the voluptuous Akilina Laptinskaya, described by a banker friend of Rasputin as a 'woman of inordinate corpulence'. Laptinskaya was something of a renaissance woman. A former nun and trained nurse, she worked for Rasputin as a secretary and financial assistant. She also took on the humbler tasks of supplying him with glasses of water and pieces of fruit. Finally, it fell to her to be ever ready, like 'Sister Maria', to relieve his tension. Police guards, supplied by the Palace, would peer, agog, through the uncurtained kitchen windows as Rasputin advanced upon her.

Laptkinskaya explained his process: 'He would be surrounded by his admirers, with whom he also slept... He would caress them... and when he or they felt like it he would simply take them into this study and do his business... I often heard his views, a mixture of religion and debauchery. He would sit there and give instructions to his female admirers. "Do you think that I degrade you? I don't degrade you. I purify you." That was his basic idea. He also used the word "grace" meaning that by sleeping with him a woman came into the grace of God.'

Reading her lucid testimony, it is tempting to cling to Laptinskaya as some kind of voice of sanity. But she had been distinctly unstable when Rasputin first met her. As a nun, she had suffered a run-in with the mad monk Iliodor, in the course of which she claimed he raped her and he claimed she seduced him. The result was that, by the time Rasputin came across her, she was confined to her cell, clutching at the walls and talking with a deep voice. Rasputin apparently restored her to her senses with the words: 'I order you to be silent.'

Another 'little lady' was Olga Lokhtina, a former St Petersburg society hostess, whom Rasputin had once cured of neurasthenia. Maria claimed her father had undergone months of celibacy before meeting Lokhtina; she had greeted him at her front door in a peignoir and he had been unable to resist her. Days after meeting him, she had forsaken her husband and daughter and followed him to Pokrovskoye. According to one account she travelled the 1,600 miles on foot.

Such was Lokhtina's devotion that she teamed a white be-ribboned dress with an unattractive wolfskin bonnet given to her by Rasputin. She passed her time chanting psalms and canticles, weighed down by twelve copies of the Gospels which she hung around her neck.

She would bring Rasputin cake, then lie on his battered sofa, while he kneaded her breasts. Their relationship at some point developed a sadomasochistic edge and he started beating her, calling her 'mad bitch' as she shouted, 'Christ is risen.' 'She won't let me alone. She demands sin,' he would protest, as she responded: 'You are God,' while yanking his penis.

When the 'little ladies' returned to Pokrovskoye 'for a little home', Lokhtina would bathe with Rasputin, his wife Praskovia and two daughters, proclaiming: 'Bad and dirty thoughts occur only to bad people.' The stolid Praskovia took everything in her stride. It was said, by Simanovich, that she and Grigory 'had a sincere friendship and never quarrelled' and her constant response to his enthusiastic 'rejoicing' was an enigmatic: 'He has enough for all.' Praskovia did once throw Lokhtina out of the house by her hair; but only because Lokhtina had called her stingy. She and Grigory both took a dim view of parsimony. The Tsar's sister, Grand Duchess Olga, complained that the Tsarina gave Rasputin sashes, crosses and patent-leather boots. His complaint was that she gave him only icons and bric-a-brac: 'It's terrible how stingy she is.' However, he did treasure one of the Tsarina's crosses, refusing to check it in at the bathhouse and preferring to stow it in the toe of his shoe with a sock.

Bishop Feofan once commented mildly that Rasputin was 'unrestrained in his treatment of the female sex... He stroked them with his hand during conversation'. Others were less reticent; the American Ambassador George T. Marye made an unfavourable comparison between Rasputin and Tiberius: 'The storied infamies of the Emperor Tiberius on the Isle of Capri are made to seem moderate and tame.' A journalist wrote grimly: 'In place of the Imperial Standard, floated Rasputin's undergarment.'

But the Tsarina was not to be distracted by what she regarded as idle chitchat. With Russia at war, she must consolidate the power of the Man of God. 'He sees far ahead, therefore his judgement can be relied upon,' she told her husband. 'Hearken unto our Friend, believe him... All my trust lies in our Friend.' She closed one letter with the confident prediction: 'a country where a Man of God helps the Sovereign will never be lost.'

She and Rasputin were increasingly thrown together while the Tsar spent more time at the battlefront. Their alliance was probably strengthened by their alienation from what might be called conventional society. The Siberian peasant and the German-born Empress were both outsiders and both, broadly speaking, unpopular. Their developing bond was already regarded with alarm by most of the Tsar's relations and a significant swathe of the Russian people. It would, in time, be regarded with deep suspicion the world over.

But there seems to have been nothing improper about the relationship. The Tsarina's unswerving devotion to her husband, 'beloved Nicky dear,' is laid bare in a torrent of passionate love letters. Unfortunately, her devotion was inflamed by a protective, motherly impulse: she believed herself smarter than he. In a letter she drew the Tsar as a babe in arms and wrote: 'Be more autocratic, my very own sweetheart... Sweety mine... don't laugh, you naughty one. It is war.'

Rasputin, as usual, echoed and re-enforced her sentiments. What he actually thought about the Tsar's capabilities remains a mystery, but he didn't mind dabbling in a bit of diablerie and disrespect: 'Papa understands nothing and cannot cope,' he wrote once, adding: 'He's afraid of everyone. He looks round to see if anyone is eavesdropping.' No wonder the Tsar began resorting to drugs: 'Hope the cocain [sic] worked well,' wrote the Tsarina.

Neither would have seen anything treacherous, however, in Rasputin's insults. The Tsarina was convinced she was operating in Russia's best interests: her love for her husband was matched by a fierce loyalty to her adoptive country. Rasputin was, as he saw it, simply strengthening the position of the brighter of 'the Tsars'.

Among the pair's early, humbler projects was stopping Rasputin's son, Dmitri, then aged 20, from going to the front. The Tsarina intervened on his behalf: 'Our Friend is in despair his boy has to go to war.' So while Romanov princes were being slaughtered in battle, Dmitri Rasputin was safely installed in Petrograd as a medical orderly.

Their next venture was infinitely more ambitious: the ousting of Grand Duke Nicholas, at that point Commander of the million-strong Russian Army. The

Tsarina wrote elaborately to her husband: 'Sweetheart needs pushing always & to be reminded that he is the Emperor & can do whatsoever pleases him – you never profit of this – you must show you have a way & will of yr. own & and not led by N [Grand Duke Nicholas] & his staff, who direct yr movements.' Rasputin, she added: 'Does not like N going with you, finds everywhere better alone... N was our Friend's enemy and brings bad luck.' For herself she added: 'I have absolutely no faith in N – know him to be far from clever and, having gone against a Man of God, his word can't be blessed.'

When the Tsar eventually capitulated, his wife moved promptly to the next nag: 'May the replacement of Nikolasha take place rapidly. No beating about the bush.' Upon hearing of the campaign against him, Grand Duke Nicholas went to Rasputin's flat and berated him, calling him an 'ungrateful pig'. After the Grand Duke stormed out, Rasputin fell to his knees before an icon, praying for those who 'spitefully use God'.

The Grand Duke's replacement, it emerged, was to be the Tsar himself. The decision proved deeply unpopular: the stout-hearted Dowager, the Tsar's mother, had already voiced her worries. She wrote in her diary on August 12 1915: 'He started to talk about assuming supreme command instead of Nikolai. I was so horrified I almost had a stroke... I added that if he did it, everyone would think it was at Rasputin's bidding, I think this made an impression as he blushed deeply!' But the Tsarina heartily approved of her husband's promotion. On September 10 1915, she wrote: 'Our Friend read their cards in time, and came to save you by entreating you to clear out Nikolasha and take over the Command yourself.'

Before departing for the front, Tsar Nicholas met his Cabinet, who pleaded with him to change his mind. Ten ministers had signed a petition registering their objection. He was sweating and clutching an icon as he rose to his feet: 'I have heard what you say, but I adhere to my position.'

Clinging to his conviction that his rule was divinely ordained, the Tsar was now as isolated as he was obdurate. He believed he must not allow himself to be swayed by his ministers: 'He... convinced himself (or perhaps was convinced by his wife) that on the day of his coronation in 1896 he had sworn to uphold autocracy,' writes the historian Richard Pipes.

A much-quoted article written by Vasily Maklakov, a conservative member of the Duma, seemed to capture the public imagination. Maklakov likened the Tsar to an incompetent driver on a dangerous road: 'The driver's slightest mistake will send the vehicle plunging down a precipice, killing all passengers. Among the passengers are capable drivers, but the chauffeur refuses to yield the wheel to them, confident that they will not seize it by force, for fear of a fatal accident.'

After reading the article, Yussoupov attempted to include the outspoken Maklakov in a plot to get rid of Rasputin. Though Maklakov did not want to be directly involved, he did supply Yussoupov with a useful cudgel. He was not against the idea of murder, even coming up with his own scheme. Rasputin, he suggested, should be knocked on the head and run over; a victim, it would appear, of yet another incompetent driver.

The Tsar had his moments of rebellion. Against the Tsarina and Rasputin's advice, he insisted upon taking the fragile Alexis to the *stavka*, his military headquarters at the front, at Mogilev. But this gesture backfired horribly on one occasion when Alexis developed a nosebleed and the pair were obliged to turn back. The attack was so bad that Alexis's tutor Pierre Gilliard thought that the boy might die. The Imperial train reversed at a snail's pace, coming to a complete halt every time the boy's bandages had to be changed.

Upon their return, Rasputin refused, for the first and only time, to come to Alexis's aid. He may have been smarting after his advice had been flouted. In any case, he gave instructions on the phone and did not appear at the Palace until the following day. Upon reaching Alexis's room, he made the sign of the cross and dropped to his knees to pray: 'Don't be alarmed, nothing will happen.' The boy's bleeding stopped, but it was later claimed that he recovered simply because one of the Court doctors had cauterised the wound. Six days later, the Tsar returned to the front alone.

At the *stavka*, the Tsar accrued a growing battery of Rasputin-abilia, forced upon him by his wife, with accompanying instructions. First there was the vial of wine, used to celebrate Rasputin's name day, January 25: 'Pour it into a glass and drink it all up for His [sic] health.' Then there was the comb: 'Comb your hair before the sitting of the ministers. The little comb will bring its help.' Finally, there was a mysterious stick topped with a fish holding a bird: 'I send you a stick wh.

was sent to Him fr. New Athos to give to you – he used it first & now sends it to you as a blessing – if you can sometimes use it, wld. be nice & have it in yr. compartment near the one Mr Ph[ilippe] touched, is nice too.'

Back in the capital, the Tsarina was increasingly left to her own devices. But she had every confidence in herself: 'Silly old wifey has trousers on unseen and was ready to lead.' And she was more than willing: 'God wishes your poor wifey to be your help, Gr always says so & Mr Ph too – & I might warn you in time if I knew things.' Rasputin was, as ever, close at hand: 'I'll ask our Friend's advice. So often he has sound ideas... Our Friend is always praying and thinking of the war.' Rasputin's thoughts could be quite specific: 'Our Friend praying and crossing himself about Romania and Greece & our troops passing through... Says no more fogg wil disturb... Khvostov (Minister of the Interior) brought your secret marche route to me and I won't say a word about it except to our Friend to guard you everywhere.'

At one point Rasputin had a useful dream: 'He saw in the night one should advance near Riga,' reported the Tsarina. Otherwise he was full of general tips such as 'firmness is a rock and wavering is death to all.' The wavering Tsar tried, to an extent, to be receptive to 'our Friend''s ideas. He was certainly witnessed by Alexis's English tutor throwing a letter from one of Rasputin's detractors in the bin: 'This is another of those denunciations of Grigory. I get them almost every day and throw them away unread.' Nonetheless, he once added a pleading postscript to one of his letters to the Tsarina:

'Please lovy mine don't mention these details to anybody. I only wrote them down for you.'

It should be remembered that the Tsarina wrote to her beloved Nicky with relentless regularity; there were many letters in which Rasputin didn't rate a mention. But the idea that the Man of God was wielding power, through the Tsarina, began to take hold. It became widely known that he was visiting her at Tsarskoye Selo; rumours were rife that ministerial appointments were being made on his say-so.

In June 1915 protesting mobs gathered in Red Square, in Moscow, calling for the Tsar's abdication: the Tsarina must be sent to a convent and Rasputin hanged. As Governor of Moscow, Yussoupov's father, 'Papa Felix', was the man responsible for quelling the riots. He made a hash of it, even boarding up shops that sold alcohol with looters still inside.

Shortly after the riots, Papa Felix went to see the Tsar, to complain about Rasputin, and was fired on the spot. Yussoupov's mother was furious at her husband's treatment, but the Tsarina remained unrepentant, repeating her maxim that her husband must have autocracy: 'M. Philippe and Grigory say so too.'

The Yussoupovs were not a family to alienate. In her memoir Maria Rasputin, described in police records as a 'peasant of Pokrovskoye village', took great pleasure in sniffing at Felix Yussoupov's credentials: 'His nobility is of recent days. The title of Prince has been in the family for two generations only.' But the Yussoupovs were at that time the wealthiest family in Russia. One estimate of their estate placed the value of their possessions, before the Revolution, at between 300 and 350 million dollars. There was so much oil on some of their land that peasants drove carts over the fields simply to grease their wheels. One year Papa Felix gave his wife a mountain for her birthday. The couple owned a gilded gondola with specially imported Venetian gondoliers and a personal train containing an aviary.

Yussoupov's furious mother, Zenaide, wrote to her son: 'Nothing can be done unless the book [the Bible, her code word for Rasputin] be destroyed and Valide [the Tartar word for Great Mother, the Tsarina] tamed.' Zenaide was used to having her own way: she kept one servant solely in charge of her muffs.

For the Tsarina, the world was now divided into 'ours' and 'not ours'. As the number of 'not ours' continued to grow, so 'ours' became more outlandish. There was the poltroonish Prince Mikhail Andronnikov, for example, a well-known conman, who now provided Rasputin with 1,500 roubles a month. Andronnikov was described, even by the forgiving Anna Vyrubova, as a 'scented person of servile behaviour and dyed facial hair'. Fancying himself a kind of churchman, the Prince installed an altar and crucifixes in his bedroom. But these symbols did nothing to quell his sexual appetite: one of his servants estimated that his master had slept with more than 1,000 young males in two years. To Mossolov, the Prince pronounced loftily: 'You know I have no official post. I might call myself ADC to the Almighty.'

In his endless round of back-scratching, Prince Andronnikov was behind Rasputin's support of two further dodgy figures: Alexei Khvostov, appointed Minister for

Internal Affairs and Stepan Beletsky, Director of the Department of the Police. Taking her lead from Rasputin, the Tsarina had added her weight behind Khvostov, writing to the Tsar: 'Please speak seriously about Khvostov to Goremykin, am sure he is the man for the moment, as fears nobody and is devoted to you.' Rasputin wouldn't have needed great accounting skills to appreciate a fat wadge of 3,000 roubles from the grateful pair.

Following a social slight, Rasputin had originally been opposed to Khvostov. He had travelled all the way to Nizhny Novgorod to speak to him on behalf of the Tsar. But Khvostov, doubting his visitor's status, had not offered him so much as a biscuit. Indeed, he sent for a policeman to accompany the Man of God back to the station. When Khvostov finally discovered who his visitor actually was and heard that, before leaving, Rasputin had sent a telegram to the Palace, he was panic-stricken and rushed to the capital to demand a meeting with the Tsar to discuss the problem of sewage in Nizhny.

Khvostov's efforts at reconciliation were so effective that Rasputin soon pronounced him a 'good man and close ally'. But that did not stop him also referring to Khvostov as 'pot-belly' and complaining about his singing at the restaurant Villa Rhode: 'You're fat and make a lot of noise.' While the Tsarina continued to support Khvostov: 'He will not let anything touch us & will do all in his power to stop attacks', she also felt compelled to mention his weight: 'His body is colossal but his soul high and clean'.

Rasputin had once been hostile to the Duma, ranting: 'There's not a single *muzhik* among them.' He would rage that the Duma members 'want to get rid of the Lord's Anointed' (by which he meant himself). There were certainly some who remained convinced that Rasputin drove through the streets in a car with blackened windows, shooting at random passers-by.

But now Rasputin seemed anxious for the Tsar to cast off his own reservations and foster better relations with the Duma. When the Duma was reconvened, on February 9 1916, the Tsar appeared in front of the assembly, at the Man of God's suggestion, and was greeted with cheers. Rasputin was pleased. As he said of the Duma members to the Tsarina: 'One cannot again uselessly offend them.'

Once prized for his stark simplicity, was Rasputin growing more clever or more corrupt? He was certainly becoming more pragmatic. 'Our Friend says that if people offer great sums [so as to get a decoration] now one must accept as money is needed,' wrote the Tsarina. She and Rasputin even decided it would be politic to mollify the hostile Duma President, Rodzyanko, with a medal: 'Our Friend says also that it would be a good thing to do... it's most unsympathetic but alas times are such just now.'

With these strategies and promotions, 'ours' hung on in the game. But Rasputin's relations with his old adversary, the Church, had been anything but straightforward. In July 1915, the Tsar had thrown a spanner in the works with his appointment of Alexander Samarin as the new leader of the Synod. Four years previously, when Rasputin had suffered his indignities at the hands of 'Blessed Mitya' and the other clerics, Samarin had demanded assurances that Rasputin remain excluded from the Church. Years later, Samarin was still insulting Rasputin, calling him a horse thief and heretic.

Rasputin complained to the Tsarina about his appointment and she, in turn, protested to her husband. The Tsar made weak attempts to defend his choice to his wife: 'Changes must happen now & one must choose a man whose name is known in the whole country & who is unanimously estimated.'

But the Tsarina was inconsolable, insisting that Samarin's promotion had reduced Rasputin to 'utter despair... His enemies are our enemies'. She accused Samarin of telling 'stories against our Friend... using vile words in speaking of him'. She wrote beseechingly: 'I am so wretched ever since I heard [the news] and can't get calm.' In August 29 1915 she told the Tsar to 'give Samarin the short order'. And on September 11: 'You must set yr. broom working & clear out all the dirt that has accumulated at the Synod.'

Instead, Samarin was setting to work with his own broom, denouncing Rasputin's coffin-loving friend, Bishop Varnava, as an unbalanced fanatic. Varnava was by this time preaching obscure sermons that the war was caused by abortion, a practice introduced to Russia by the Germans. The Tsarina defended him stoutly: 'Bishop Varnava comes from the people... he understands them.' Samarin's more serious complaint was that Varnava had conducted an important religious ceremony, a laudation, without Synod approval. The Tsarina had no time for such excuses: 'Samarin intends getting rid of him [Varnava] because... he is good to Gr.'

Varnava was summoned by the Synod to Petrograd. While the hostile churchmen sat cross-legged, smirking and catcalling, Varnava was forced to stand. He had brought the Tsar's telegram giving him permission to sing the laudation. The telegram did nothing to appease his accusers. The Tsarina, outraged, leapt to Varnava's defence, telling her husband that he 'should hurry with clearing out Samarin as he & Synod intending to do more horrors and he [Varnava] has to go there again, poor man, to be tortured'.

The unsuspecting Samarin went to the Tsar's military headquarters to complain about Varnava, only to discover that he himself had fallen from favour: the Tsar asked him pleasantly about his family, then ordered the elderly Goremykin to call him from the dining table and tell him he was fired.

That same day, Alexander Volzhin was appointed head of the Synod. Volzhin had been suggested by 'pot-belly' Khvostov, and came with the endorsement of the Tsarina: 'He made me a perfect impression... one sees he is full of the best intentions and understands the needs of our Church perfectly well.' Her support had been assured after he asked her to bless him: 'wh. touched me very much'.

The Tsarina was momentarily satisfied with the Synod, particularly when she was presented by its members with a Testimonial and Image in recognition of her work with war victims: 'Since Catherine, no Empress personally received them alone. Grigory is delighted.' Rasputin himself had been gratified when, on his last birthday, in January 1916, a speech was delivered in the Synod celebrating his importance for the State.

But the new leader, Volzhin, did not prove so well intentioned as the Tsarina had hoped. He had serious reservations about Rasputin's protégés. Aside from the troublesome Varnava, there was Pitirim, who had once installed his male lover in a mansion and was later to be accused of stealing 100,466 roubles from a monastery. Ministers were already boycotting his liturgies at St Isaac's Cathedral and Rodzyanko had railed at him: 'Rasputin and men like him must be expelled and your own name cleared from the opprobrium of being looked upon as a nominee of Rasputin... Your Eminence, your very looks betray you.' Yet Pitirim prided himself on his forbidding looks; some of his followers swore he had a halo.

Then there was Isidor, who had become a bishop in 1909, only to be stripped of his rank, two years later, for sodomising a lay brother. Rasputin had been behind his restoration as a bishop earlier in the year; his faith in Isidor was matched by the Tsarina, who wrote on October 1 1916 that she had spent a 'quiet peaceful' evening with Brother Grigory and Bishop Isidor: 'We talked so well & calmly – such a peaceful harmonious atmosphere... Had a nice evening at A's [Anna Vyrubova's] yesterday – our Friend, His son & the bish Isidor.'

All three bishops were doing suspiciously well. Varnava stood to be promoted to Archbishop within months and Pitirim had been made Metropolitan of Petrograd, an appointment endorsed by Khvostov and Anna Vyrubova, for which Rasputin mysteriously received 75,000 roubles. Isidor, arguably most powerful of all, was now installed at Tsarskoye Selo as the Tsarina's favourite. When she heard of Volzhin's disapproval of the bishops, she was furious, dismissing Volzhin as 'a coward & frightened of public opinion'; he was 'too pompous' and 'quite unfit' to lead the Synod.

Under Volzhin's influence, the number of Synod members who were 'not ours' was growing. Heated discussions were held over who would hold the Synod's number two position. Rasputin suggested Prince Nicholas Zhevakov, a mystic who had been visited by a vision in which the Russian Army was victorious after bringing a certain icon to the front. The Tsarina promptly wrote to her husband: 'Rasputin finds you ought to tell Volzhin you wish Zhevakov to be named his side.' The Tsarina liked to lend authority to Rasputin's tips by substituting 'finds' for 'thinks'.

But Rasputin found, instead, that Volzhin had had enough. In the summer of 1916, Volzhin asked to be relieved of his post. Rasputin and Pitirim immediately came up with a replacement: a short, be-wigged man called Nicholas Raev. Raev had served in the Ministry of Education, but his most recent enterprise had been a high-stakes gambling club. The Tsarina extolled the virtues of pupils at a school that operated under his auspices: 'His girls behaved beautifully' at a time when 'there were rows in all the schools and universities'.

The Tsarina met Raev on June 27 1916 and found

him an 'excellent man'. Racv and Rasputin talked for more than an hour, after which Rasputin pronounced him 'a real Godsend'. Raev was duly appointed head of the Synod on August 20 1916, with the mystic, Prince Zhevakov, as his assistant.

The ructions created by the Tsarina and Rasputin in the Synod were reflected in the Government. The months leading up to the Revolution saw four different prime ministers, five ministers of the Interior and four ministers of agriculture. Rasputin had at various points been behind the appointments of Khvostov, as Minister of the Interior, Raev, as leader of the Synod and Beletsky, as Director of the Department of Police. The Tsarina's words had borne some fruit: '9 Sept 1915... Clean out all, give Goremykin new ministers to work with & God will bless you & their work.'

In fact, as an advisor and recommender of candidates Rasputin proved increasingly unreliable. His ever failing 'gift for knowing people' led to his frequently changing his mind and, on at least one occasion, recommending two rival candidates for the same government post.

On January 20 1916 Boris Sturmer replaced the elderly Goremykin as Prime Minister. The good news for the Tsarina and Rasputin was that Sturmer was as much 'ours' as Goremykin. Nevertheless, Sturmer, at 69, was only nine years younger than Goremykin and Rasputin was no respecter of age: 'He's old, but he'll do.' While regretting the departure of Goremykin, the Tsarina was gratified that Sturmer 'very much valued Gr which is a good thing.'

But Rodzyanko denounced Sturmer as 'an utter nonentity'. The new American ambassador, David R. Francis, was exasperated by Sturmer's habit of looking in the mirror and twirling his moustaches during meetings. Sturmer's moustaches were indeed remarkable, immaculately turned up and appearing to act as hooks to a lavish tongue of a beard. The French Ambassador Paleologue described him as a 'false Father Christmas with moist red lips and a crafty smile, curiously repellent' and insisted that Sturmer had been chosen 'on account of his insignificance and servility'.

Paleologue's evaluation was borne out by Rasputin's threats: 'If I say the word they'll kick the old guy out' and 'Sturmer had better stay on his string or his neck will get broken.' Any attempt to break free of his string was met with a rebuke: 'Don't you dare go against Mama's wishes.' As it turned out, Sturmer never went against Mama's wishes, even taking upon himself, years later, the onerous task of burning Rasputin's files.

For all his inadequacies, Sturmer also took on the job of Foreign Minister. The controversy surrounding his over-promotion was occasionally noted even by the Tsarina, who once suggested that he should take some time out: 'Protopopov and our Friend both find for the quiet of the Duma, Sturmer ought to say he's ill for three weeks.' But she had been unable to stomach the preceding Foreign Minister, Serge Sazanov, particularly mistrusting his good relations with Paleologue and the British Ambassador, George Buchanan, and finally dismissing him as 'long-nosed' and a 'pancake'.

The widely esteemed Minister of War, Alexei Polivanov, was next to go: 'Is he not our Friend's enemy?' demanded the Tsarina. Polivanov had objected to Rasputin's having access to four high-powered war office cars, all of them too fast to be trailed. The Tsarina grew impatient with her husband: 'Lovey don't dawdle, make up your mind, it is far too serious.' When Polivanov finally fell, the Tsarina was momentarily appeased: 'Now I shall sleep well.' Polivanov's replacement was a die-hard monarchist, General Dmitri Shuvalev, who was obsessed with footwear, turning every conversation to the whys and wherefores of boots.

The most controversial of the Tsarina and Rasputin's campaigns, however, was for the promotion of Protopopov. In September 1916 the newly appointed Minister of the Interior was hissed at and jeered when he appeared in the Duma wearing an outlandish uniform that he had designed himself. He was inclined to sob and was addicted to the sinister Tibetan Dr Badmaev's powders for male potency. But the Tsarina was only interested in Protopopov's attitude to Rasputin. Protopopov had established some sort of friendship with Rasputin; but he was sufficiently nervous of public opinion to visit the flat in thick dark glasses. The Tsarina wrote that Protopopov 'likes our Friend since at least four years' and 'Grigory begs you earnestly to name Protopopov there... His love for Russia & you is so intense.'

When the Tsar had finally agreed to promote

Protopopov, the Tsarina was jubilant: 'Our Friend says you have done a very wise act in naming him.' She wasted no time, once Protopopov was in place, in making use of him: 'Our Friend begged for you to speak of all these things to Protopopov.' The new Minister of the Interior embraced his power with gusto. Among his first projects was the orchestratration of letters from the Russian people to the Tsarina containing, as Gleb Botkin put it, 'extravagant expressions of unbounded loyalty'. Protopopov insisted to an unreceptive Rodzyanko: 'I feel that I alone can save her [Russia].'

The Imperial Court Director, Mossolov, was once obliged to have a three-hour meeting with Protopopov, during which he read files while the Minister talked, jumping from subject to subject. As Mossolov recalled: 'I could see plainly that I had to deal with a lunatic.' He subsequently described Protopopov to the Tsarina as 'a muddle-headed person' and was gratified by her response: 'We so rarely hear the truth from anyone.' But in October 1916, she showed no sign of believing Protopopov to be muddle-headed, writing to her husband: 'Sturmer and Protopopov both completely believe in our Friend's wonderful, God-sent wisdom.'

In desperation, Mossolov sought Rasputin out at Gorokhovaya Street, with the intention of ordering him to stop meddling in the promotion of ministers and, specifically, to oust Protopopov. The oddly matched companions drank three glasses of Madeira in silence, before Mossolov felt sufficiently braced to issue his unwelcome orders. During the ensuing discussion Rasputin had several fits of pique: 'If that's it, I'll pack my bags and go; I see I'm no longer wanted here... Do you think Papa and Mama will let you do what you like?'

As it happened, the Tsar already had some sympathy with Mossolov's view: 'Our Friend's ideas about people are sometimes queer,' he mused to his wife, even before the promotion. He agreed with Mossolov that Protopopov 'jumps from one idea to another and can't stick to one subject'. After expressing new doubts about the Minister to his wife, he now begged 'please don't mix in our Friend'. But 'mixing in' was, of course, unavoidable: the Tsar was soon in receipt of a 238-word telegram from Rasputin; the Man of God warned, confusingly, that, without Protopopov, he would be like a turnip without teeth.

'Mama' visited the military headquarters in order to plead Protopopov's cause and the Tsar, of course, backed down. This would have been a particular bone of contention for yet another prominent minister, Alexander Trepov. The Tsar had managed to make an uncharacteristic, unilateral decision to remove Sturmer as Prime Minister and replace him with the capable Trepov. But Trepov had agreed to take the appointment only on condition that Protopopov was fired. The Tsarina was livid: 'I could hang Tr for his bad counsels... Trepov does not trust me and our Friend.' Trepov was to last 47 days as Prime Minister.

he baneful influence of the Man of God was undoubtedly being felt within the Government and the Synod. But, for every one of his small successes, Rasputin was paying a hefty price. His star was falling, and the 'wasps', as he called his enemies, were multiplying.

Ever wilder rumours were circulating to the effect that he had slept with both the Tsarina and Anna Vyrubova and that, before taking to bed, he would have his boots pulled off and his feet washed by the Tsar. Cartoons were beginning to be published of the Tsarina cavorting with Rasputin; schoolchildren sang lewd songs. The most damaging story was that Rasputin had raped the four young Grand Duchesses and that the girls were now mad with lust. Rasputin's reply to all these accusations was brief: 'Nobody fouls where they eat.'

Playing cards were printed with Rasputin's face replacing the Tsar's on the King of Spades. A black market flourished, selling police notes detailing his activities. To staunch the unending gossip, hostesses would have to put up signs: 'We don't talk about Rasputin here.' According to Meriel Buchanan, the daughter of the British Ambassador, those who did discuss him were afraid to mention his name directly, calling him simply 'the nameless one'. The Duma member, Vladimir Purishkevich, who would later conspire with Yussoupov, distributed 9,000 photographs of Rasputin carousing with the disgraced Bishop Isidor.

The Tsar's ever more implacable relations, the Grand Duke cousins, made no secret of their suggested remedies: the Tsarina must be sent to a convent and Rasputin to Siberia. The Tsar, they added, should be deposed and Tsarevich Alexis crowned in his place. The Tsarina's sister, Ella, widow of the murdered Grand Duke Sergei, joined the clamour, making a special visit to the Palace. The Tsarina responded by reaching for the phone and requesting a carriage to take her sister away. As Ella later said: 'She drove me away like a dog.' Yussoupov's doughty mother, Zenaide, complained to the Tsarina and she too was sent off with a flea in her ear.

At Easter 1916, when Rasputin was back in Pokrovskoye enjoying a little 'home' time, the Tsarina wrote to her husband: 'Thought so much of our Friend and how the bookworms and pharisees persecute Christ.' Rasputin's last trip to Pokrovskoye had begun well, as he was seen off from Petrograd by Munia and Olga Lokhtina 'with basketfuls of squawking chickens'. But it ended in a furore as detectives were forced to break up a spat between him and his father, Efim, after he had given the elderly man a black eye for calling him an 'ignorant old fool who only knows how to fondle Dounia's soft parts'. Rasputin also suffered injuries, and developed an awkward gait. One of the agents watching him reported that 'Rasputin sidles.'

Coincidentally, Efim died soon afterwards, but Rasputin made no effort to sidle to the funeral. He claimed grandly that he sent his son, Dmitri, to the requiem mass, 40 days after the burial, 'since I myself had to remain behind at the Tsars' request'.

By the time Rasputin returned to Petrograd, his enemies were seeking to discredit him by any means possible. In autumn 1916 they blamed him for the halting of an important military offensive. He had indeed tried to stop the campaign and was pleased when the Tsar appeared to be obeying his instructions. '23rd Sept... Our Friend says about the new orders you gave to Brusilov etc "Very satisfied with father's orders, all will be well,"' wrote the Tsarina. 'He won't mention it to a soul.' In fact, the campaign, which cost more than a million Russian lives, simply 'ran out of steam', as the historian Richard Pipes puts it.

Rasputin's image was repeatedly tarnished by reports that he was acting as a spy for the Germans. His closeness to the Tsarina, by then known as 'Nemka', the German one, was raised as an important factor. The British Ambassador, Buchanan, talked to his French counterpart Paleologue of 'a hotbed of teutonic intrigues at the Palace'. Yussoupov had once seen Rasputin with five men, 'unmistakably Jewish in appearance', and taken them for 'an assembly of spies'. It did not help that Rasputin met Ignaty Manus, a German banker, every Friday over a period of several months. Manus had paid Rasputin for his appointment as an actual state councillor and the pair were sufficiently friendly to go out carousing. On May 26 1915 one of Rasputin's guards wrote: 'Rasputin came home drunk in Manus's car.' Manus was believed by Paleologue to be a German agent.

Attempts on Rasputin's life were once again on the increase. He was almost run over several times. On one such occasion, timber was tipped in front of his car, after which he proclaimed: 'They'll kill Mama and Papa also.' Officers with sabres set upon him in a bar when he asked a girl to dance. In a repetition of the strange episode with Maria's fiancé's frozen fingers, he apparently paralysed these officers with a glare.

One mysterious plot involved a female singer friend of Rasputin, who received an anonymous telephone call from a man promising to provide for her daughter if she would join a conspiracy. Intrigued, the singer agreed to meet the man at a club. Throughout the meeting, the man wore a mask. Many believed the masked man to have been Grand Duke Alexander, 'Sandro', the husband of the Tsar's sister, Grand Duchess Xenia.

Turncoat friends proved particularly deadly. 'Pot-belly' Khvostov, on discovering that the fickle Rasputin had withdrawn his support and was now opposing his promotion, immediately joined the growing band of detractors, citing as his reason a curious piece of skullduggery. He claimed that the Man of God had boasted at a party that he was sleeping not just with the Tsarina but also with her eldest daughter, Grand Duchess Olga. When challenged, Rasputin had reached for the telephone, pretending to call Olga. A young prostitute had duly appeared, her fur-trimmed coat convincing the other guests, 'country bumpkins', that she was indeed royalty. 'This incident persuaded me that Rasputin had to go, to save the Motherland,' declared Khvostov.

In no time, Khvostov's partner, Stepan Beletsky, also switched sides. By early 1916, the slippery twosome had recognised that their best prospects lay in getting rid of

Rasputin. Khvostov later said Yussoupov's mother, Zenaide, had told him she had unlimited funds available for this purpose, while Beletsky had apparently been offered 200,000 roubles by another of Rasputin's enemies. Khvostov first tried to persuade Rasputin to go to a monastery, promising him 8,000 roubles and several bottles of Madeira. Rasputin pocketed the money, but fought his way out of a carriage as the door was being closed.

Soon Beletsky and Khvostov had recruited the head of Rasputin's bodyguard, Colonel Mikhail Kommisarov, to help them. The treacherous Colonel enjoyed trying to disarm Rasputin by saying: 'Stop the holiness, talk sense and have a drink.' Khvostov suggested strangling Rasputin and burying his body on a frozen river bank, to be washed away in the spring thaw. But Kommissarov disagreed, preferring poison, which he duly tested on Rasputin's cats. Discovering his beloved cats dead, Rasputin was furious. He blamed Prince Andronnikov and demanded his exile to a remote town.

In the spirit of endlessly shifting loyalties, Khvostov and Beletsky themselves now fell out. When word got round that Khvostov had been trying to contact Rasputin's deadly old foe, Iliodor, Khvostov rushed to assure Anna Vyrubova that he was innocent of any murder plot: if anyone wanted to kill Rasputin, it was surely Beletsky. 'He wept and said the whole story was a blackmail,' recalled Anna. Iliodor, incidentally, was doing his bit: he planned to fly over the frontline and drop thousands of copies of his book, *Rasputin the Holy Devil*.

The Tsar finally dismissed both Khvostov and

Beletsky in March 1916. For the Tsarina, it was good riddance; she offered a rare acknowledgement of her faulty judgement: 'Am so wretched that we, through Grigory, recommended Khvostov to you – it leaves me no peace – you were against it and I let myself be imposed upon by them.'

Khvostov and Beletsky were now out of the frame, but the growing opposition was unrelenting. Verbal attacks upon Rasputin in the Duma continued, and rose to a head in November 1916, with the leader of the Constitutional Democrats quoting an article published in a Swiss paper which suggested that Rasputin had been behind many recent ministerial appointments in Russia.

Felix Yussoupov, the Tsar's flamboyant nephew, had been emerging as the unlikely leader of the increasingly desperate anti-Rasputin faction within the Romanov family. He was present at the Duma for this speech, and clearly found the article all too plausible.

Nearly three weeks later, he heard the fiery Purishkevich also speaking passionately in the Duma, alluding to those 'dark forces' invoked by Guchkov four years earlier: 'If you are loyal to your sovereign... go to the Imperial Headquarters, throw yourself at the Tsar's feet and... plead with the Sovereign that Grishka Rasputin be not the leader of Russian internal public life.'

Grand Duke Nikolai Mikhailovich lined himself up with the wasps: 'If it isn't in your power to remove those influences from her [the Tsarina] then at least protect yourself from the constant meddling,' he wrote in protest to the Tsar. In response, the Tsarina huffed that the

Grand Duke should be sent to Siberia. As she wrote: '4 November... He & Nikolasha [Grand Duke Nicholas] are my greatest enemies in the family, not counting the black women [Militza and Anastasia]... Wifey is your staunch One and stands as a rock behind you.'

She also showed the Grand Duke's offending letter to Rasputin: 'On reading Nikolai's letter He said: "Nowhere does Divine grace show through, not in a single feature of the letter, but only evil... The Lord has shown Mama that all that is worthless, asleep".'

At around this time Yussoupov wrote to his mother: 'We seem to be living on the slopes of a volcano and the same thoughts lurk in all our heads.' He tried to enlist the support of the British Embassy chaplain, the Rev Mr Lombard, by then a longstanding friend. Over tea he asked the chaplain to talk to the Tsarina: 'He suggested my trying to contact the Empress, on the score of certain knowledge of the Occult lore which I happened to possess. I told him that to supplant R. [Rasputin] would be hopeless and also that probably the Ambassador would have a good deal to say if I attempted to interfere.'

The broadminded padre, as he was known, would not have been disturbed by tales of Yussoupov's own excesses. As his grandson wrote: 'His interest in the spiritual, combined with a most sympathetic and gentle nature made him a wide circle of acquaintances in Russia.' But, with all his generosity of spirit, the padre retained, for the rest of his life, an unforgiving view of the Russian temperament: 'From the Tsar to the meanest peasant, the only thing they understand is the knout.'

Yussoupov's failure to persuade the padre to help

'supplant' Rasputin did not deter him. His nervous excitement had been increased by some particularly wild claims about the Imperial couple made recently by Rasputin. Rasputin had reported that the Tsar was regularly 'given a tea which causes divine grace to descend on him. His heart is filled with peace, everything looks good and cheerful to him'. He also said that the Tsarina was planning a coup d'état: she would be acting against her husband, on the grounds of his ill health, and was about to declare herself Regent until the Tsarevich came of age.

Yussoupov felt a grand role taking shape. With Grand Duke Nicholas, Grand Duke Alexander and his parents, he was convinced that Rasputin must go. He would have been particularly swayed by the Tsarina's sister, Ella, who was a nun and a close friend. Their belief was that Rasputin's presence at Court was blackening the reputation of the Imperial family and would soon lead to revolution. His presence had already proven itself a threat to Russia's internal stability; it was now damaging the country's reputation abroad.

The British diplomat Samuel Hoare, then head of the Russian bureau in Petrograd, had no hesitation in laying all of Russia's problems, in late 1916, at Rasputin's door. He wrote: 'Let the Emperor only banish this man and the country would be freed from the sinister influence that was striking down its natural leaders and endangering the success of its armies in the field.'

Years later, the leader of the Provisional Government, Alexander Kerensky, was equally adamant about Rasputin's detrimental role: 'Without Rasputin there would have been no Lenin.' A survey conducted between January and May 1917 by a Duma committee, based on the reports of its provincial agents, confirmed Kerensky's view. It concluded 'that the spread of "licentious tales and rumours" about Rasputin and the "German Empress" had done more than anything to puncture the belief of the peasantry in the sacred nature of the monarchy'.

It is clear that Yussoupov had wanted for some time to be the man ridding the Court of this troublesome peasant. However, at some stage in the proceedings, he began coveting a more central, and more glamorous role: as assassin.

The French Ambassador, Paleologue, was disparaging about Yussoupov's motives for disposing of Rasputin: 'Felix has regarded the murder of Rasputin mainly as a scenario worthy of his favourite author Oscar Wilde.' In her memoir, Maria Rasputin also invoked Wilde with reference to Yussoupov, insisting that the Prince had been corrupted by his three years as an undergraduate at University College, Oxford. In the land of Oscar Wilde and 'Bosie', she wrote, he had fallen for 'the more inviting college of Sodom'.

Prince Yussoupov had always relished being centre stage. As a toddler he would demand: 'Isn't Baby pretty?' At 12 he dressed himself up as a girl, in a wig and his mother's pearls, before singing at St Petersburg's Aquarium club. He was rumbled only when one of his mother's friends recognised the jewellery. His father was horrified, calling his son 'a guttersnipe and a scoundrel'. The young Felix enjoyed knockabout japes, once getting his dog drunk and allowing it to pee on guests. On another occasion he dressed it in wig, face paint and powder, before propelling it into the drawing room, where his mother was talking to a priest. Later, when travelling to England, he circumvented quarantine laws by dressing his bulldog as a baby.

Yussoupov never quite got over his prettiness. As an adult he was tall, clean shaven and still pretty; with neat features and a delicate mouth curled upwards at the corners in a cynical smirk.

He and Rasputin first met in 1909; the Prince had been unimpressed. The Man of God had, in turn, dismissed Yussoupov as a 'frightened schoolboy'. As he said to his ever loyal Munia: 'He needs help or the devil will gobble him up for dinner.'

But Munia was not to be influenced by either party against the other. She was a lifelong friend of the Yussoupovs, but she was also in the thrall of Rasputin for eight years. Her own relationship with Rasputin had been initiated through her passion for Yussoupov's luckless older brother, Nikolai, who had been killed, aged just 26, in a duel. After his death, she had tried desperately to contact him through clairvoyants and had then resolved to lock herself away in a convent. Rasputin seemed to answer both these needs.

Seven years after their first meeting, Yussoupov was still critical of Rasputin. He thought Rasputin changed, his face more flabby and puffy. But his main preoccupation, throughout this second meeting, on November 20, was Rasputin's disrespectful attitude towards Munia. They met at Munia's house, and Yussoupov was disgust-

Prince Youssoupov had always relished being centre stage. As a toddler he would demand: 'Isn't Baby pretty?' At 12 he dressed himself up as a girl, in a wig and his mother's pearls, before singing at St Petersburg's Aquarium club.

ed when he saw Rasputin kissing his hostess on the lips. He wrote that he ached to crush Rasputin like an insect. When Munia invited him to sit down and take tea, he didn't deign to answer, simply asking, as usual, whether he had received any phone calls.

At their first meeting, Yussoupov had kept his distance from Rasputin; now he had to make intimate overtures. He told Rasputin he wanted to be cured of his homosexuality, as it was affecting his marriage. Munia testified that he was also 'complaining of chest pains'. Finally, the Prince said that his wife was in need of treatment for some mystery ailment and Rasputin pressed him for details. Throughout their discussion, the Man of God was full of good will, declaring: 'There's no trash with me.'

Munia cheerily insisted that Rasputin would love to hear Yussoupov play the guitar. Continuing in the vein of revelry, Rasputin asked Yussoupov to accompany him to the gypsies, as he would say: 'With God in thought but with mankind in the flesh.' But Yussoupov refused to commit himself, saying he had to prepare for his Military College exams. When Rasputin suggested Munia accompany him instead, her mother expressed her horror. Rasputin rounded on her: 'What are you cackling about?'

He seemed preoccupied, as usual, by the phone. When it rang, he barked at Munia: 'I expect that's for me. Go and see.' Having spoken on the phone, he returned, out of sorts. It emerged that he had been discussing the controversial Protopopov, probably with Anna Vyrubova. After several further calls, he appeared to have won his case. As he told Munia later: 'After I'd shouted a bit they calmed down...'

Yussoupov's next meeting with Rasputin was at the flat in Gorokhovaya Street; he and Munia were dropped at a discreet distance away. Rasputin himself welcomed them at the door: 'You've come at last. I've been waiting.' Yussoupov disapproved of the flat décor, sniffily noting paintings badly executed and a general feel of 'bourgeois wellbeing and prosperity'.

The two men were left alone after the Man of God snapped at Munia: 'Go into the other room.' By way of a conversational gambit, Rasputin sneered at the Duma, evidently forgetting his intention not to 'uselessly offend' members. He now dismissed them as 'dogs collected to keep other dogs quiet', adding over-optimistically that 'their babblings won't last much longer'. He boasted to Yussoupov: 'Say the word and I'll make you a minister,' and unnerved him by taking his hand and saying: 'Don't be afraid of me.'

Both parties seemed to enjoy a certain theatricality. But how clear were they about their ever-changing roles? Rasputin, increasingly the fearful victim, was playing, once again, the mover and shaker at the heart of Government. Yussoupov, masquerading as the tremulous patient, was steeling himself to play murderer.

There was no doubt that Yussoupov, once the St Petersburg flâneur, had become an intriguer. He was confounding detractors with his new sense of purpose, not least the Tsar's younger sister, Grand Duchess Olga, who in the past had spoken disparagingly of the: 'utterly unpleasant impression he makes, idling at such times'.

After Yussoupov's visit, Rasputin reverted to tragedy, writing plaintively to the Tsar: 'I shall be killed. I am no longer among the living.'

The Tsarina was, as usual, immersed in her own scenario. On November 2 1916 she wrote: 'Anxious about Baby's arm so asked our Friend to think about it.' On December 4, by which time Rasputin was in imminent danger, she told her husband to have 'more patience and deepest faith in the prayers and help of our Friend'. And a few days later she urged him to 'rely on Rasputin's wonderful brain – ready to understand everything'.

Prince Felix Yussoupov spent the snowy day of December 16 adding finishing touches to an elaborate *mise en scène*. An empty wine cellar at his sumptuous palace on the Moika Canal had been converted into a dining room. The room was freshly painted and decorated: new curtains were hung, doors nailed in place and electric wiring installed. Lavish furniture was brought from other rooms, including carved wooden chairs, porcelain vases and a bearskin rug.

The table was laid as though a dinner had just taken place, with smeared plates, used cutlery and scrunched-up napkins. Drops of tea were poured into the teacups and half-eaten cupcakes strewn alongside place settings on the table at which, as Yussoupov pronounced proudly, 'Rasputin was to have his last cup of tea'.

In the afternoon, Yussoupov took himself off

through the blizzard to the Kazan Cathedral, to pray for two hours. Convinced of the justice of his mission, he would have enjoyed an inspiring session, unaware that his victim had visited the cathedral days before. After attending to his spirit, Yussoupov visited the Military Academy; he intended to take his exam the following day.

He had three main fellow conspirators. Vladimir Purishkevich was the Duma member whose recent speech had so impressed Yussoupov. He was known for several idiosyncrasies, not least throwing water at his adversaries and cocking a snook at the Socialist element by sporting their symbolic red carnation in his fly buttons. It fell to Purishkevich to procure chains heavy enough to carry a body to the bottom of the Neva River. That fateful day he spent several nervous hours working at home, before venturing out to attend the Duma.

Purishkevich was 46, balding, with a full black beard and pince-nez. He had been immediately taken with what he saw as Yussoupov's 'indescribable elegance and breeding' and was clearly enamoured of the romance of the murder plot. Later, describing the stage set of a cellar, he noted excitedly that it resembled an 'elegant bonbonniere in the style of ancient Russian palaces' and that 'the pink and brown petits fours were chosen to complement the colour of the walls'.

The second conspirator was Grand Duke Dmitri, the Tsar's cousin, who was aged just 25 and also striking, with large, plaintive, hooded eyes. Purishkevich described him as a 'handsome, stately young man'.

And the third was Dr Stanislaus Lazovert, a friend

of Purishkevich: an army doctor, he had worked in a hospital train run by Purishkevich. Among Lazovert's tasks was the preparation of one of Purishkevich's hospital cars, to be used to transport the body to a hole in the ice next to the Petrovsky Bridge. Lazovert spent hours tinkering with the engine, though not very fruitfully as it turned out: during its brief mission, the car kept stalling. He painted over an identifying 'semper idem' ('always the same') emblem on its side.

Dr Lazovert's primary role, however, was to provide the cyanide, which he cut up and sprinkled into wine glasses and cupcakes. He created a setback during the preparations when he threw his rubber gloves into the fire, filling the room with smoke. He later passed out and had to be revived in the snow. But at this early stage of the proceedings, he readily prepared himself for the role of chauffeur. By 11.00pm he had dressed up in a suitable coat and peaked cap. He collected Purishkevich and the pair arrived at Yussoupov's splendid Moika Palace at the same time as Grand Duke Dmitri.

Purishkevich and Dr Lazovert were both no doubt acting altruistically, taking personal risks in order to right what they perceived to be a terrible wrong. Purishkevich had publicly expressed his fierce disapproval of Rasputin, but he may have been as beguiled by the conspiracy's drama as with its justice. Dr Lazovert's motives remain less clear; but, by this time, it was of course a commonly held belief that Russia would be better off without Rasputin.

Grand Duke Dmitri and Yussoupov were very close. It was rumoured that the pair had once been lovers and that Dmitri, in a jealous rage, had tried to kill himself. Yussoupov, though happily married, was known never to have been averse to what he called 'love affairs of a special kind', and Dmitri, though once betrothed to the eldest Grand Duchess, Olga, certainly wrote Yussoupov highly emotional letters: 'How desperately I long at times to have a talk with you... For God's sake write to me... I must again restrain my urgent desire to see you.'

Rasputin, incidentally, was not as fond of the Grand Duke as he was of Yussoupov. He claimed that Dmitri had a skin disease so contagious that the Imperial children were told to wash their hands with a special solution after touching him.

Shortly before midnight, Dr Lazovert drove Yussoupov to Gorokhovaya Street to collect Rasputin. The late pick-up was unusual, but its peculiarity had not particularly struck Rasputin. He may have been more than usually befuddled by the prospect of meeting the stunning Princess Irina.

Dr Lazovert's later statement that, at this point, he entered Rasputin's flat is not borne out in any other account. His other claim regarding Rasputin's feelings during his last drive – 'Rasputin was in a gay mood' – is equally contentious. Yussoupov had no recollection of Rasputin being either gay or, as Maria claimed, slightly apprehensive. In fact, he was unnerved to find Rasputin completely calm and exhibiting nothing at his reputed 'gift for knowing people'. Once the pair arrived at the Moika Palace, he helped Rasputin off with his overcoat: 'I looked at my victim with dread as he stood before me, quiet and trusting. What had become of his second sight?'

What were Yussoupov's own feelings that night? It has been claimed that he had some sexual fixation with Rasputin. Yussoupov's description of the trances into which he was put by Rasputin definitely have a sensuous relish. It was widely acknowledged that the Man of God's eyes were mesmeric and that he could expand and contract his pupils at will. Yussoupov gave a graphic account of one of Rasputin's so called 'cures': 'His hypnotic power was immense. I felt it subduing me and diffusing warmth throughout the whole of my being. I grew numb; my body seemed paralysed. I tried to speak, but my tongue would not obey me, and I seemed to be falling asleep, as if under the influence of a strong narcotic.'

Maria was adamant that during the course of their meetings over the previous month, Yussoupov had been trying to seduce Rasputin. Watching the two of them avidly at the flat, she once caught Yussoupov ostentatiously drinking from the same side of a glass as her father. She also recalled her father telling her of an occasion when he had found Yussoupov lying naked on his broken sofa during what was supposed to be a treatment session for his homosexuality. 'There is no doubt what he had in mind. Papa was dismayed to find that all his efforts were in vain.'

Any sexual advance would have been particularly

contrary. Yussoupov never tired of listing Rasputin's unattractive traits, describing him as having 'a mincing gait' and walking around 'bending, squatting, rubbing his hands'. He talked of Rasputin's 'untidy tangle of hair' and his face 'of the more ordinary peasant type – a coarse oval with large ugly features overgrown with a slovenly beard and with a long nose'.

Of his qualities as a healer, Yussoupov was no less critical, saying he had 'no trace of spiritual refinement' and was prone to 'mutter incoherently'. But then his general repugnance need not have deterred him: the Prince was known for being perverse.

For his part, Rasputin was clearly drawn to Yussoupov; his name for him, 'The Little One', was blatantly affectionate if not sexual. One of the Tsar's cousins was insistent that Rasputin was in the grip of a 'carnal passion' for Yussoupov.

Later, describing the events of that fateful night, Purishkevich would reveal his conviction that something had happened between Yussoupov and Rasputin when they were left alone together in the cellar. He reported having heard a suggestive groaning sound or, as he put it in French, a *gémissement*. Years later, Yussoupov seemed to incriminate himself, revealing all sorts of intimate details about Rasputin's sexual attributes to Duff Cooper. At what point he had acquired this knowledge is unclear. Yussoupov claimed to Duff Cooper that Rasputin could withhold orgasm for prolonged periods and that he had three large penile warts.

Accounts vary as to that evening's exact sequence of events. But Yussoupov's and Purishkevich's versions are similar enough to have been accepted as true.

Yussoupov first settled Rasputin at table, amid the after-dinner clutter, explaining to him that the guests had adjourned upstairs with the beautiful Princess Irina. Rasputin's meeting with the Princess, he said, could take place as soon as these others had left. To give the illusion of a party above, the conspirators planned to play gramophone records. Sadly, at some late stage, they discovered that the Yussoupovs had only one record: 'Yankee Doodle Dandy'.

The Prince had also prepared to play some music himself: against the cellar wall, he had carefully propped his guitar. Yussoupov was known for singing and playing gypsy songs; he and Dmiri performed duets. Rasputin perked up when he spotted the guitar. 'Play something cheerful,' he demanded, later adding: 'You have much soul in you.' Otherwise the pair shared desultory conversation, during which they discussed 'mutual friends'. In one account Yussoupov claimed that he tried to persuade Rasputin to leave Petrograd.

Rasputin may not have been suspicious of Yussoupov, but nor was he inclined, initially, to be convivial. He turned down ever more insistent offers of poisoned food and alcohol. When he finally did eat and drink, he showed no ill effect. Yussoupov began to suspect that his victim was being protected by supernatural powers. Increasingly unnerved, he left the room three times to complain to his conspirators upstairs. Purishkevich remembered Yussoupov's words: 'The poison's effect is apparent only in the fact that he keeps belching and there seems to be an increase in saliva.'

In exasperation, Grand Duke Dmitri, the least committed, suggested they abandon the plot altogether. But he was overruled by the others. They all now agreed that their only option, with the failure of the poison, was to shoot him. All four ventured downstairs together, but, as they were creeping down, Yussoupov snatched Grand Duke Dmitri's gun, announcing that he wanted to carry out the assassination himself. He went on ahead and found his victim gazing, enraptured or dazed, at a 17th-century bronze and crystal crucifix. When Rasputin made some appreciative comments, Yussoupov admonished him: 'Grigory Efimovich, you would do better to look at the crucifix and pray.' As soon as Rasputin began praying, Yussoupov shot him, point blank, in his side.

Claims that the conspirators, now a full two floors up, heard Rasputin's body landing on the white bearskin rug seem unlikely. What the conspirators did hear, however, was Rasputin's 'wild scream' as he was shot. All three rushed down to see what was happening, but, as they entered the room, one of them either flicked the light switch or tripped on a wire and the room was plunged into darkness. Yussoupov said he froze in terror, lest he step on his victim. A few minutes later, the lights came back on and they surveyed the crumpled body on fhe floor.

Although Purishkevich had spoken out against Rasputin in the Duma so vociferously, he had never actually set eyes on him. He wondered now how this so-called Man of God could have influenced the destiny of Russia: a peasant *si banal et si odieux*. The rattled Grand Duke was the first to speak; he told the others that, to avoid stains, they must get the body off the bearskin rug and onto the stone floor. After moving him, the conspirators switched off the lights, locked the door and went upstairs.

But Yussoupov, it seems, couldn't resist returning to the cellar. Half an hour later, he crept back downstairs and peered closely at the corpse. He swore that, at that point, Rasputin came back to life: 'First one eye, then the other, opened with a look of diabolical wickedness.' The Man of God now lunged at Yussoupov, 'bellowing and snorting like a wild animal'. In the ensuing scuffle, Rasputin tore off one of Yussoupov's epaulettes: 'It seemed that the devil himself, incarnate in this muzhik [peasant], was holding me in vice-like fingers never to let me go.'

Upstairs, Purishkevich heard Yussoupov's '*cri sauvage, inhumain*'; both attacker and victim were now screaming like animals. Grand Duke Dmitri and Dr Lazovert had left the palace to burn Rasputin's clothing, though, confusingly, none of it was ever burnt. Purishkevich had been relishing a moment of quiet, with a celebratory cigar, when he heard the terrible commotion downstairs. He rushed, spluttering, into the corridor and collided with Yussoupov, who barged past him and ran into his parents' quarters

There were disputes about whether Purishkevich did, in fact, fire the fatal shot. It was mooted that Grand Duke Dmitri (above), a trained soldier, was the more likely candidate.

shouting: 'He's alive! He's getting away.'

Purishkevich leapt downstairs, drawing a gun from his pocket. Rasputin had by now somehow heaved himself through a gate and into the palace yard, and was running at speed through the snow yelling: 'Felix, Felix, I'll tell the Tsarina everything.' Purishkevich ran after him and fired two shots, but they both missed. In a desperate bid to help himself focus, Purishkevich then bit his own left hand and fired a third shot which he claimed killed Rasputin.

There were disputes about whether Purishkevich did, in fact, fire the fatal shot. It was mooted that Grand Duke Dmitri, a trained soldier, was the more likely candidate. The Tsar's eldest daughter, Grand Duchess Olga, was in no doubt that it was her former fiancé. She wrote in her diary: 'We have learned that Father Grigory has definitely been killed, it must have been by Dmitri.'

There is also evidence, however, that the *coup de grâce* was fired by a British secret service agent. The idea is not so outlandish. The Tsar and George V were cousins: the Man of God had become an embarrassment for the British as well as the Russian monarchy. But the more urgent concern would have been the widely held notion that Rasputin was somehow lobbying for a separate peace with Germany.

The agent most frequently referred to as the assassin was Oswald Rayner, a friend of Yussoupov's from Oxford. He had visited the Moika Palace several times during November; he was with Yussoupov the morning after the murder and for the next 24 hours. Another British agent said shortly afterwards that 'awkward questions were being asked.' The Tsar later told the Ambassador, George Buchanan, that he had heard that British officers were involved. Buchanan's insistence that the allegation contained 'not a word of truth' did nothing to quell rumours. It is said, even now, that King George V was involved.

Alternative rumours were rife. Bertie Stopford, an English friend of the Tsar's cousins, was in close contact with Yussoupov at the time. He was told that Rasputin had been given a gun and ordered to shoot himself. Perhaps the least likely suggestion put forward was that Rasputin was shot by Yussoupov's Ethiopian servant, Tesphe, a man so unsophisticated that he liked to peer into lavatories to watch the water flushing.

In the early hours of the morning of the 17th, Purishkevich persuaded two soldiers to help him drag the body inside. He then searched for Yussoupov, finding him in a bathroom, trembling, spitting and vomiting. Purishkevich led him to the stairs above where the body was lying, so that he could see that Rasputin was actually dead. Yussoupov peered over the bannister and glared at the body, before throwing Maklakov's cudgel at it. He then ran downstairs and set about beating it. In the end Purishkevich – puzzled by the passionate ferocity of Yussoupov's attack – had to order the two soldiers to pull him off.

Yussoupov was by now finally convinced that Rasputin was dead, but, at that moment, Purishkevich began to entertain his own doubts. He maintained that he saw and heard Rasputin still showing signs of life: 'Turning his face up, he groaned and it seemed that he rolled his right eye which fixed me, dazed but terrible, I see it before me now.'

A spanner should have fallen into the works when the police called, after hearing shots at 3.00am. But Yussoupov somehow managed to fob them off, telling them he had been holding a party and that Grand Duke Dmitri had shot the porter's dog for fun. In the course of the evening Yussoupov had, indeed, shot his dog as a way of accounting for blood in the snowy yard. He later complained: 'Because of that reptile I had to shoot one of my best dogs.'

The ebullient Purishkevich couldn't resist bragging to the police that they had murdered Rasputin. But the police were unsure whether to take him seriously. Two days later, Yussoupov, still sticking to various false accounts, attempted to be breezy about Purishkevich's 'confession'. 'I had a telephone conversation with Purishkevich about this matter and he explained that he had said something about Rasputin to the policeman, but because he had been very drunk he could not remember what exactly.' In fact, for all his eccentricities, Purishkevich was a member of the Temperance League.

The conspirators wrapped Rasputin's body in his coat and a blue curtain, before loading it into the car and driving to the Petrovsky Bridge. Purishkevich had an uncomfortable journey, complaining that his 'knees touched the repulsive, soft corpse'. He added that the 'body kept jumping about, despite a soldier sitting on top of it.' While the body was heaved over the parapet into the river, Grand Duke Dmitri kept watch. As Purishkevich said: 'The Royal youth must not touch the criminal body'.

At some point Yussoupov recovered himself sufficiently to send a telegram to his wife in the Crimea: 'It's all over.' Purishkevich also sent a telegram, to Maklakov: 'When are you coming?' – the code message for 'Rasputin has died.'

There was a further call from the police between 7.30 and 8.00. The police seem to have been singularly ineffective during these crucial hours; they may have been thrown by the presence, at the palace, of not just one but two members of the Imperial family. In any case, it was only now, during this second visit, that they conducted a proper inspection, discovering telltale bloodstains in the cellar. Yussoupov's curious attempts to cover traces of blood with scent had evidently been unsuccessful. But, in his memoirs, Yussoupov failed to mention the police discoveries, stating simply that, after recovering from his attack of nerves, he managed to remove brown stains from floors and carpets with the help of his manservant.

The next day, the Rasputins' maid, Katya, woke Maria and Varya to tell them that their father hadn't returned. The telephone wires were soon buzzing.

Maria rang Anna Vyrubova; Rasputin's niece, Anna, rang Munia; Maria rang Yussoupov, but he said he knew nothing. When she told him he had been spotted at the flat, he claimed he'd taken Rasputin to the Villa Rhode restaurant. This would have been all too plausible; Rasputin never tired of ringing 'Alphonse' to book tables, which would duly be prepared with flowers and fish.

But when Maria rang the Villa Rhode, she was told that nobody had seen her father. Maria then got a call from Protopopov who had himself had a call from the Mayor of Petrograd enquiring about Rasputin's disappearance. Yussoupov and Grand Duke Dmitri both rang the Palace in a bid to defend themselves from rumours already circulating about their involvement. But the Tsarina refused to speak to either of them. She said of Yussoupov coldly: 'Let him write.'

The Tsarina wrote an agonised letter to her husband at the military headquarters. 'We are sitting here together – can you imagine our feelings – thoughts – our Friend has disappeared... Felix [Yussoupov] pretends he never came to the house and never asked him... I can't and won't believe he has been killed. God have mercy. Such utter anguish.' She added ominously: 'Felix came often to him lately.'

With the prescience of a natural hysteric, the Tsarina soon had a good idea of the truth, writing to her husband the next day: 'No trace yet... the police are continuing the search. I fear that these two wretched boys (Yussoupov and Grand Duke Dmitri) have committed a frightful crime but have not yet lost all hope.

Start today, I need you terribly.' The Tsarina was particularly distressed about the involvement of Grand Duke Dmitri: 'whom I loved as my own son'.

Grand Duchess Olga wrote in her diary: 'Father Grigory has been missing since last night. They are looking everywhere. It is terribly hard. The four of us [the young Grand Duchesses] slept together. God help us!' The Tsar himself took the news of Rasputin's disappearance differently. He is said to have walked away whistling.

Yussoupov may initally have denied any involvement in the murder to the police and the Tsarina, but he was not so circumspect with his friend, the Rev. Mr Lombard. After turning up at the chaplain's house, he threw himself on a sofa, and pronounced: 'Padre, we have done it.'

Unfazed by Yussoupov's flagrant disregard of his earlier advice, the chaplain agreed to accompany him to the scene of the crime, where he insisted on blessing the cellar with holy water and incense. He was always to remember the blood on the white bearskin carpet: 'I cannot describe the horror of the atmosphere. It felt filthy and unclean, the only other place where I have experienced the same feeling was in the Museum at Scotland Yard. I gained his consent to cleanse that room ceremonially.'

Less than 24 hours after watching her father leave

Gorokhovaya Street with Yussoupov, Maria found herself having to identify one of his galoshes. The boot was one of the pair hidden by Maria and her sister in their vain attempt to stop their father leaving the night before. It was brought to the flat by a policeman, accompanied by Rasputin's disgraced friend, Bishop Isidor.

The identification process was described baldly in a police report: 'The brown size 10 shoe, manufactured by Treigol'nik, found under Petrovsky Bridge, on the River Neva, has been presented to Maria and Varvara [Varya] Rasputin. They confirmed that the shoe belonged to their father; it was the right size and looked the same.'

Rasputin's body was finally discovered two days later, on the morning of December 19, after a sleeve of his fur coat had been spotted protruding from the ice on the Neva. The Rasputin sisters were taken, with Anna Vyrubova, to view their father's body. 'The face was almost unrecognisable: clots of dark blood had coagulated in the beard and hair; one eye was almost out of its socket and on the wrists were deep marks left by the bonds that my father had succeeded in breaking in his death struggle,' wrote Maria with her usual candour.

The initial pathology report from Professor Dmitri Kosorotov was equally gothic; the autopsy had been conducted by the light of oil lamps and a lantern. 'His left side has a weeping wound, due to some sort of slicing object or sword. His right eye has come out of its cavity and falls down into his face... The victim's face and body carry traces of blows given by a supple but hard object.' The pathologist was shocked by the extent of Rasputin's head injuries. The 'goat like expression and enormous head wound [were] hard even on my experienced eyes'.

There were disputes as to whether there was water in his lungs. If water was found, it would have proven that Rasputin had still been alive when thrown into the river and that he had, in fact, drowned. But that would give rise to a fresh problem: saints, it was believed, could not drown. Why had the divine force that protected Rasputin from poison and bullets not protected him from drowning? This particular worry should have died with the confirmation that there was no water in the lungs.

A photograph exists of the body on a sledge, having just been pulled from the Neva. His raised hands became the subject of much debate. Some believed, like Maria, that Rasputin had somehow retained the strength to free his arms. Others maintained he had miraculously come back to life, before breaking his bonds. The more fervent 'Rasputinki' believed he had raised his hand in a sort of benediction.

Maria's emotional turmoil at the time was exacerbated by further questions from the police about the exact nature of her father's relationship with the Tsarina. The police had been told that she had once found the pair in bed together; her silence had been bought with a bracelet. She convinced the police that the story was untrue with an unlikely burst of laughter.

Five days after her husband's disappearance, Praskovia, their son Dmitri and the faithful Dounia reached Petrograd. Maria had sent a telegram to Pokrovskoye to say that her father was missing. When

Praskovia arrived at the station and saw her daughters' black clothes, she knew at once that her husband was dead.

When the 'frightful crime' was confirmed, the Tsarina was inconsolable. The children's tutor, Pierre Gilliard, was horrified by the effect of his death upon her: 'Her agonised features betrayed... how terribly she was suffering... They had killed the only person who could save her child.' The immediate reaction to Rasputin's death of the children, to whom he had once been so close, was not recorded in any detail, though Grand Duchess Olga was heard to say: 'I know he did much harm, but why did they have to treat him so cruelly?'

The initial plan to bury Rasputin at Pokrovskoye was shelved after fears were raised that his corpse would be attacked en route. It was judged wisest to bury him on land which, though close to the Alexander Palace, was not the property of the Imperial family. He was given a ceremonial burial just before Christmas, on December 21, in a chapel still in the process of being built by Anna Vyrubova. The proceedings had been planned in great secrecy, with those attending strictly limited to the Imperial family and a handful of retainers. No members of Rasputin's family were invited, an oversight neither forgotten nor altogether forgiven by Maria. Of Rasputin's 'little ladies', only the voluptuous Laptinskaya attended.

His grave was marked with a wooden cross. Months earlier there had been a service marking the laying of the chapel's foundations. 'Our Friend and nice Bishop Isidor there,' the Tsarina had reported gaily.

Anna Vyrubova arrived for the service in a carriage with inappropriately jingling bells. The Tsar, Tsarina and their four daughters drew up in a motor car; the Tsarevich, Alexis, was ill and could not attend. The Tsarina wept at the sight of the coffin. The Tsar's diary entry demonstrated that, for all his whistling, he had not taken the murder lightly: 'At 9.00 o'clock we went to... the field where we were present at a sad scene: the coffin with the body of the unforgettable Grigory, killed on the night of the 17th by monsters in the Yussoupov house.'

The Romanovs' lively priest, Father Vassiliev, conducted the service. Bishop Isidor continued the singing, after his fellow miscreant, Bishop Pitirim, found himself overcome with emotion.

The Imperial family were in deep mourning that Christmas. There were no presents and the Tsarina wept for hours at a time. 'I can do nothing but pray & pray & our Friend does so in yonder world for you,' she wrote to the Tsar.

She may have found consolation from Protopopov's claim that he was in regular communion with Rasputin. Protopopov became the Tsarina's new '*homme de confiance*'. Liberals who had once loathed Rasputin now hated Protopopov. At a New Year's Day celebration, Protopopov offered his hand to Rodzyanko, who spat: 'Nowhere and never.'

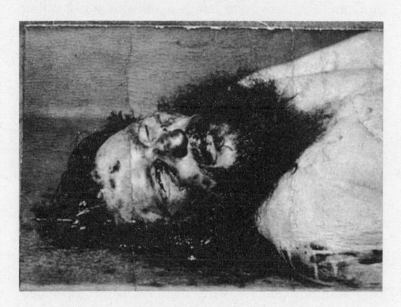

Rasputin's body was finally discovered two days later, on the morning of December 19, after a sleeve of his fur coat had been spotted protruding from the ice on the Neva.

The punishment of Rasputin's murderers proved problematic. The 12-year-old Tsarevich Alexis protested to his father: 'Is it possible you will not punish them? Stolypin's assassins were hanged.' But this was a rather more awkward case, one which highlighted, once again, the rift which Rasputin had created among the Tsar's relations. Sixteen Romanovs signed a petition opposing the Tsar's decision to punish Grand Duke Dmitri. Two days after the murder, the Tsarina's own sister, Ella, had sent Grand Duke Dmitri a congratulatory telegram: 'May God give Felix strength after the patriotic act performed by him.'

Yussoupov was feted as a hero. Though he had his own reservations, the British diplomat Samuel Hoare reported jubilantly that 'all classes speak and act as if [Rasputin's death] is better than the greatest victory in the Russian field'. *The Times* printed photographs of Yussoupov and his wife, Princess Irina, captioned 'Saviours of Russia'. The *Manchester Guardian* leader on the death of Rasputin was resolute: 'Few men so well known have had so little good said about them, and if a fraction of what has been said against him be true, Russia will be a better place without him.'

The Prince would find people kneeling and crossing themselves outside his palace. There were cheers in factories, with workers passing resolutions to protect him. Photographs of the assassins decorated shops. Yussoupov was accosted by Rodzyanko, who said, 'Moscow wants to proclaim you Emperor. What do you say?'

The Tsarina's sister, Ella, claimed that nuns at a

certain convent had gone mad with glee, shrieking and blaspheming. Jubilant sisters ran along the corridors as though possessed, howling and lifting their skirts.

In the end, the Tsar, perhaps mindful of his wife, decided to exile both Yussoupov and the Grand Duke, proclaiming: 'No one has the right to commit murder.' Yussoupov was to be sent to one of his family's far-flung estates, while the Grand Duke was dispatched to Persia.

In the first weeks of 1917, the Tsarina found solace at Rasputin's graveside: 'Went to our Friend's grave... I feel such peace and calm when I visit his dear grave.' She continued issuing instructions to the Tsar: 'Wear his cross, even if it is uncomfortable, for my peace of mind.'

By February 1917, however, events in Petrograd had spun out of control. Opposition had been growing to Russia's involvement in the war and rumours of impending bread shortages triggered a panic reaction among the populace. Textile workers went on strike; they were joined by tens of thousands more strikers who then took to the streets.

On February 28 the city was at a standstill and the Tsar was cabled at the front by one of his desperate ministers: 'The Government, never having enjoyed Russia's trust, is utterly discredited and completely powerless to deal with the grave situation. Further delays and vacillations threaten untold misfortunes.'

The Tsar finally agreed, in anguish, to abdicate on March 2. Days later, rebel soldiers found and desecrated Rasputin's grave, relieving themselves on the site and writing on the wall: 'Here lies Grishka Rasputin, shame of the House of Romanov and the Orthodox Church.' They dug up the coffin, hoping to find jewellery. Rasputin's saintly aspirations had not protected him from decomposition: his corpse stank and his face was blackened.

He was reburied secretly by Provisional Government soldiers but then dug up again, stowed in a piano box and driven down the Old Petersburg Highway, destined for a third burial site. But, in a manner foreshadowing the fate of the corpses of the Imperial family, the vehicle carrying the piano box broke down and it was decided to burn the body at the roadside.

On March 11, at seven in the morning, the corpse of the Man of God was set alight. The fire burned for two hours and, at one point, the body appeared to rise up out of the flames. One reason for this may have been that the soldiers who burned him had no experience of cremating and failed to cut his tendons. When the tendons contracted in the heat, the body gave the appearance of sitting up. In another of his fortuitous prophecies, Rasputin once told a journalist: 'If they do burn me, Russia is finished; they'll bury us together.'

Maria claimed that, after her father's death, she and her sister Varya visited the Palace regularly. Though they had not been invited to their own father's funeral, the sisters were now warmly welcomed by the Tsarina, who assured them: 'The Tsar is your father now.' But the visits began to peter out when three of the young Grand Duchesses caught measles and completely stopped after the Imperial Family's house arrest. On Maria's final visit, the Tsarina reached into a large jar in the hall and presented her with a handful of butterscotch balls.

When the Tsarina heard that the captive Imperial family was to be taken to Siberia, she firmly believed they were following 'our Friend'. On August 1 1917 she wrote a strangely buoyant letter to Anna Vyrubova: 'My sweet beloved Precious childy... one does not tell us where we go (only in the train shall we know) nor for how long – but we think it is where you and ours were last summer – our Saint calls us there & our Friend – wonderful is it not?'

On their way, the family travelled in a steamer, *Rus*, from Tyumen to Tobolsk and all seven gathered on the deck as they sailed past the village of Pokrovskoye. Rasputin's two-storey house loomed above the other simple huts. His shadow continued to haunt them, as their guard in Tobolsk, Vasily Pankratov, testified: 'He removed the last vestiges of the halo from the Tsar's family. He was constantly drunk here, on drunken business, he pestered women with dirty propositions.'

But the Tsarina was indifferent to the guard's disapproval. On the anniversary of Rasputin's death, she wrote in her diary: 'The terrible 17th. Russia too suffers for this, all must suffer for this.'

Eight months later, on their way to what would be their final resting place, Ekaterinburg, the Tsar and Tsarina found themselves, under guard, actually stopping in Rasputin's village. On April 27 1918 the Tsarina wrote: 'About 12, got to Pokrovskoe, changed horses, stood long before our Friend's house, saw his family & friends looking out of the window.'

The predicament of the Imperial couple was, by this time, critical. The Tsarina, as usual oblivious, wrote: 'Com [Commandant Yakovlev] fidgety, runing [sic] about, telegraphing.' The desperate Commandant had, in fact, heard of several plans to attack the party, to 'disarm us in order to seize the baggage' ('the baggage' being the Tsar). It happened, once again, as Rasputin had predicted: 'Willing or unwilling they will come to Tobolsk and they will see my village before they die.'

A month after the Tsar and Tsarina travelled to Ekaterinburg, glimpsing the Rasputins for the last time, the Tsarevich Alexis followed with three of his sisters. On May 22 1918, their ship docked at Tyumen where Maria Rasputin happened to be at the pier, in the course of a home visit, buying tickets. She spotted two of the Imperial family's retainers with Alexis, waving through a dirty window: 'They were like angels.'

Maria Rasputin had, by this time, followed her father's bald instruction, 'Love Boris', by marrying, in 1917, a graduate of a school of mysticism called Boris Soloviev. During the last few months of the Romanovs' captivity in Ekaterinburg, Soloviev tried to rescue them with the aid of 175,000 roubles from a monarchist banker in Petrograd. At one point, he insisted that 300 officers were ready to storm the house in which the family were held captive: 'Grigory's family and his friends are active,' he wrote. But the plans came to nothing and indeed some kind of skullduggery was suspected when several of his fellow conspirators were arrested.

The Imperial family were allowed out twice a day, for half an hour, in a small garden surrounded by a 14-foot board fence. The Tsarina joined in the walks until the guards started taunting her about Rasputin. During the family's last days alive, graffitti appeared on the walls depicting 'Grishka' and 'Sashura' (the Tsarina) having sex. Lewd comments were added about the size of Grishka's penis.

On the night of July 16 1918, nineteen months after Rasputin's murder, the Imperial family were shot and bayoneted to death. The murders confirmed yet another of Rasputin's prophecies: 'If any of the Romanovs [are] involved in my killing... none of you... will remain alive for more than two years.' One of those involved in his murder had, of course, been the Grand Duke Dmitri.

In the Tsarina's trunk, Bolshevik guards fell upon a red silk shirt, blue silk trousers and tasselled silk belt belonging to Rasputin.

Rasputin once said to Yussoupov: 'Disaster will come to anyone who is against me.' This prediction was, to some extent, borne out. The Black

Princesses, Militza and Anastasia, and Grand Duke Nicholas survived the Revolution. All three escaped with the Yussoupovs on the British battleship, HMS *Marlborough*, in 1919. But they all lived reduced lives in exile. Grand Duke Nicholas and Anastasia spent their last days together in a tiny villa in Paris before moving to Cap d'Antibes. The Grand Duke died, aged 73, in 1929, and Anastasia, aged 67, in 1935. Militza was persecuted by the Germans while living in Italy during the Second World War. She died in Egypt in 1951.

The bull-like Rodzyanko fled to Serbia in 1920 but died in poverty four years later; Dzunkovsky was executed by Stalin, in 1938, at the Lubyanka. The conniving 'pot-belly' Khvostov and Beletsky were killed by Bolsheviks in 1918. Prince Andronnikov and the Tibetan healer Badmaev were killed the following year. The dreaded Iliodor, once charismatic leader of thousands, spent his last years as a janitor at the Metropolitan Life Insurance Building in New York. He died in the Bellevue Hospital in 1952.

Bishop Hermogen died a martyr's death in Tobolsk in 1918. Bolshevik soldiers forced him to roll stones naked up a river bank, while prostitutes jeered and insulted him. His persecutors tied a huge stone to his neck and lowered him by his hair into the river. When the White Army arrived, they exhumed his corpse. It was untouched by decay, but for a missing section of beard.

Rasputin's assassins did not do so badly. Apart from Purishkevich, who died of typhus while fighting for the Whites in 1920, they all survived the Red Terror. The only rain in Dr Lazovert's life fell, years later, when he returned from holiday to find a restaurant called 'Rasputin' opening directly opposite his apartment in France. Settling finally in Romania, the former doctor became an oil trader. He wrote his own account of Rasputin's murder, but this was discounted by many as 'mere fiction'. On his deathbed he insisted that he had substituted the poison for some harmless substance.

Yussoupov and his wife, Princess Irina, escaped from Russia with two Rembrandts and a stash of jewellery. They so mismanaged their accounts, however, that they were soon penniless, struggling even to buy light bulbs. At a particularly low point, they were in New York selling their jewels, when they were announced, at a party, as Prince and Princess Rasputin.

But in the end it was their connection with Rasputin which secured their fortune. In 1932, MGM released *Rasputin And The Empress*, in which a character closely resembling Princess Irina is ravished by Rasputin. The Yussoupovs sued for libel, and were awarded $750,000 or $15 million in today's money. They subsequently enjoyed a thoroughly pleasant existence, mostly in the South of France. Yussoupov fancied himself a faith healer, spending hours at a time in hospitals and sanatoriums. He and his wife both enjoyed painting grotesque pictures of Rasputin-like faces complete with grimaces.

He was courted by Hitler, whose envoy pronounced that he would be the best candidate for the Russian throne. After the publication of two memoirs in the 1950s, *Lost Splendour* and *En Exil*, the Soviets offered him an exile in Russia, but Yussoupov dismissed both of these approaches out of hand.

Yussoupov dined out on his gory story, getting quite nettled if a social event went by with no mention of the murder. In a ring on his finger, he wore one of the bullets that had hit Rasputin. Oswald Rayner, the British Secret Service agent mooted by some as Rasputin's killer, also boasted a bullet in a ring.

It was with such burlesque details that the Rasputin myth continued to flourish. Speculation regarding his sex life was rife. And it was soon asserted, in smart British circles, that he had enjoyed sexual relations with Yussoupov. As Noel Coward wrote: 'The truth I think is that Rasputin had a tiny little lech on Yussoupov himself.' Yussoupov died in Paris, aged 81, in 1967.

Grand Duke Dmitri was also feted. He himself felt very torn as to whether he had done the right thing. When he saw his father the day after the murder, he denied any involvement, giving his word on an icon and on a photograph of his dead mother. He was mortified by the acclaim thrust on him and once walked out of a theatre in Petrograd, to avoid the embarrassment of an ovation. He would not have welcomed the news that, in the weeks following the murder, crowds were lighting candles around St Dmitri, at the Kazan Cathedral. He finally broke down with a *crise de nerfs* on the train taking him from Petrograd to his exile in Persia.

He and Yussoupov fell out of touch, only running into each other, some years later, at the Ritz Hotel in London. The Grand Duke had heard someone singing and playing a guitar in an adjacent room, and correctly identified the singer as his old friend. As Yussoupov wrote: 'I thought it was an irritated neighbour but it was Grand Duke Dmitri, who I had not seen since "l'affaire Rasputin". He had recognised my voice through the door.'

The pair resumed their friendship until Yussoupov published his first lurid memoir, in 1927. Grand Duke Dmitri considered it a breach of their agreement not to discuss the murder in public. As he said in a Russian paper published in Paris: 'Not a single person, including the members of my own family, has heard from me about the events of that terrible night... The same force that impelled me to the crime has prevented me and now prevents me from lifting the curtain on that affair.' He never spoke to Yussoupov again. Grand Duke Dmitri died in Switzerland in 1941, aged 49, of TB.

For all Rasputin's pronouncements, disaster seemed, in the end, more likely to befall his supporters than his detractors. Of his bishops, Varnava and Isidor were murdered; Pitirim died in 1920. As for his 'little ladies', Laptinskaya disappeared, while Lokhtina was driven to take refuge in Makari's mud hut. The elderly Goremykin was caught by a mob and strangled on Christmas Eve of 1917. Sturmer was arrested by Bolsheviks and died in the Peter and Paul Fortress the same year. Protopopov fled from the ministry with a briefcase containing the Tsarina's letters and photographs of Rasputin's corpse. He had only two years of communing with Rasputin's soul before he himself was killed by Bolsheviks.

Rasputin's friend, the jeweller Simanovich, reached the US but was rendered penniless by the Depression; he lost his sickly son, before he himself died, destitute and alone. Anna Vyrubova had a long but lonely life as a Russian Orthodox nun in Finland. She lived in her own apartment, surrounded by pictures of the Tsar, Tsarina and Rasputin. She died in 1964, aged 80.

Rasputin's faithful wife, Praskovia, son, Dmitri, and younger daughter, Varya, fared particularly badly. At the time of his death, Rasputin's estate was valued at a relatively modest 23,507 roubles and 66 kopecks: roughly £54,000 in today's money. This included 5,092 roubles and 66 kopecks cash in the Tyumen State bank. His house was valued at 10,000, and 8,000 roubles-worth of property included a 500-rouble fur coat, a 700-rouble gold watch and 900-rouble silver tea service. The Rasputins' farm animals comprised two cows, a bull, eight sheep and eight horses, with a stud worth 1,000 roubles. In the days before the Revolution, the Tsarina had instructed Protopopov to give the Rasputins 100,000 roubles, but this instruction was never carried out.

In November 1919, the fabled grand piano and gramophone were confiscated. Eight months later, the Rasputins were stripped of their furniture, mirrors and even dishes. In June 1920, Praskovia, Dmitri and his wife were expelled from their home: as the owner of ten long-horned cattle, Dmitri was denounced as a wealthy farmer, a kulak. In 1933, Dmitri's wife and a daughter died of TB; three months later he himself died of dysentery. Praskovia outlived her son by three years, dying in 1936, aged 69, with just 76 roubles and 40 kopecks to her name. Varya worked as a stenographer and tried, at one point, to escape to Germany but was stopped at the border carrying the manuscript of a memoir. She was dispatched to a Soviet prison where she apparently died from poisoning in 1924 or 1925.

Only Rasputin's daughter Maria survived into old age; though her long life was distinctly checkered. She and her husband Boris Soloviev, the mystic who had failed to rescue the Romanovs, fled to Vladivostok in 1919. There Boris began a fraud involving courtesans pretending to be the surviving Grand Duchesses. Businessmen would give money to kiss the hand of these 'Grand Duchesses' and watch sorrowfully as the women boarded a steamer into exile. The courtesans would then scuttle down another gang plank, to be safely back on land before the final whistle blew.

The Solovievs fled next to Romania, then to Germany, with two daughters. The marriage was not a great success: Maria swore she could never 'love Boris' while he confided to his diary that he found many women more attractive than his wife. Boris surrounded himself with a group of supporters trying to contact Rasputin's soul, before he himself died in 1926.

Maria, then 28, became a governess in Paris, before joining a circus troupe with which she toured Europe and the US, billed as 'the daughter of the famous mad monk whose feats in Russia astonished the world'. She worked as a lion tamer for the Ringling Brothers Circus and was mauled by a bear in Peru, Indiana. There followed a short period of domesticity, during which she lived in California with her daughters, Maria and Tatiana, and their family dogs, Yussou and Pov.

When Yussoupov published his memoir she tried to have him arrested for murder: 'To me it is atrocious and I do not believe that any decent person could help feeling a sentiment of disgust in reading the savage ferocity of this book.' She vainly claimed $800,000 in damages. Her plea for sympathy was undermined by the shameless ferocity of her own books.

In 1960, she claimed that a rouged homosexual with dyed hair had visited her daughter's house in Paris and had from there telephoned Yussoupov, saying: 'You'll never guess where I'm calling from.'

In August 1968, aged 70, Maria met the fraudulent Grand Duchess Anastasia, Anna Anderson, whom Yussoupov had already dismissed as a 'frightful play actress'. After the meeting, in Charlottesville, Virginia, Maria suffered a sleepless night, insisting that she had been reunited with her childhood friend: 'Bless God it is [she] but it is such a decision. I am afraid almost to think about it... it gives me the chills.'

She returned to Charlottesville three months later to persuade 'Anastasia' to accompany her back to California. She and her friend, Patte Barham, had co-written a biography of her father; they hoped the presence of a grand duchess would boost sales. Anna Anderson initially agreed, but then changed her mind. To console themselves, the pair spent the evening letting their hair down in a bar.

Fifty years earlier Maria had scoffed at policemen in Petrograd when they had suggested she had caught her father sleeping with the Tsarina. Now she was boasting that this was exactly what had happened. Maria and Patte left town the following day; by the time they reached Dulles Airport, in Washington, Maria was denying she had ever recognised Anastasia.

Gleb Botkin, the son of the Imperial family's doctor, who believed Anna Anderson to be the real Anastasia, was relieved: 'A Rasputin gives the case a bad name.' Gleb's opinion of Maria had not changed since he had denounced her as an unsuitable playmate for the Imperial children at Court. He now described her as 'a very homely Siberian peasant with the small eyes of a sly pig and saccharin manners of very doubtful sincerity'. Maria Rasputin died in Los Angeles in 1977, aged 79.

The St Petersburg hostesses who banned talk of Rasputin in the early 1900s would have been horrified to know that, a hundred years on, the tongues have not stopped wagging. The public's appetite for history's 'mad monk' will, it seems, never be sated.

Maria Rasputin was not slow in coming forward with her own contribution to the Rasputin legend. She wrote three sensational memoirs of her father: *The Real Rasputin* in 1929, *My Father* in 1934 and *Rasputin the Man Behind the Myth* in 1977.

In 1990, her co-author Patte Barham used her interviews with Maria to flesh out her *Peasant to Palace: Rasputin's Cookbook*, which features 'Marzipan Tart

Romanov' and 'Grand Duke's Bouillabaisse' alongside humbler recipes gleaned from Rasputin's timorous mother, Anna. Maria had claimed that the Court adopted several simple dishes and that the Tsar's first choice was 'Rasputin's Jellied Fish Heads'. She further insisted that her father ascribed his singular sex drive to a basic codfish soup:

'Rasputin's Codfish Soup':
Makes 3 to 4 servings

1 small whole codfish
1 cup whole milk
1 cup heavy cream
salt and pepper

Clean codfish; remove head (use for 'Jellied Fish Heads', if desired). Cut into fillets and remove bones; cut fillets into pieces and place in heavy saucepan. Add milk and cream. Place over medium heat and bring to scalding temperature; DO NOT BOIL. Reduce heat and continue simmering until fish is done. Season to taste with salt and pepper. Ladle into soup bowls and serve hot.

These four books, written or inspired by Maria, form a small brick in a pantheon of literature, operas, documentaries and feature films about Rasputin.

Lionel Barrymore starred in the controversial *Rasputin And The Empress* in 1932; Christopher Lee starred in the Hammer Horror *Rasputin: The Mad Monk* in 1966. Tom Baker took the role of Rasputin in the film of Robert K. Massie's book *Nicholas and Alexandra* in 1971. Alan Rickman won an Emmy for his performance in *Rasputin: Dark Servant of Destiny* in 1996 and the most recent film, *Raspoutine*, starred the hulking French actor, Gerard Depardieu. Talks are now being conducted with Leonardo DiCaprio.

In 1978, the pop group Boney M brought out their single 'Rasputin', with its chorus 'Ra Ra Rasputin, Lover of the Russian Queen'. It went to Number Two in the British charts and has since become a disco mainstay. An initial ban on the song in the USSR was eventually lifted and it is claimed that Boney M once performed the song at a museum in Pokrovskoye. Boney M fans also point out that the group's lead singer, Bobby Farrell, died, spookily, in the same city and on the same date as Rasputin. Farrell did, indeed, die in a hotel in St Petersburg in 2010 and though the date, December 30, seems wrong, it is technically correct since, in 1916, the Russian calendar was 13 days behind the Western calendar.

The face of Rasputin has appeared on vodka and beer labels. The murder cellar, for many years a lavatory, has been re-created as a tourist destination, presided over by semi-convincing models of Youssoupov and Rasputin.

Kyril Zinovieff and his elder sister, both aged over 100, are now, in 2013, probably the last two people alive to have seen Rasputin. Kyril remembers as a young boy going for a walk in St Petersburg with his nurse and sister. He saw a cab draw up close. 'Two big black bears of men were inside the cab. One was laughing his head off. His hat was off, his head was back. I could see his teeth gleaming between his black moustache and black beard. I asked my nurse who he was, she replied that it was Rasputin. I said: "Who's Rasputin?".'

Zinovieff was told that Rasputin was immensely important. His parents were friends of the Yussoupovs: 'Felix harped on about Rasputin's influence. He and his parents believed Rasputin was the real ruler. I was brought up on that. My father said the Emperor was weak. One of the Galitzines even believed that Rasputin had an office in the Winter Palace.'

He believes that Yussoupov exaggerated his role with regard to the assassination: 'Felix saw himself as the saviour of Russia.' But recognising Yussoupov's limitations has not dented Zinovieff's affection for him: 'He was amusing. He sang gypsy love songs and had a nice voice. During his libel court case, he retired to a room and played guitar. He was not an intelligent man.' Zinovieff is dismissive of Yussoupov's belief in Rasputin's mystical power: 'That's all nonsense'... All Rasputin could do was alleviate the suffering of Alexis.'

He may be loosely in agreement with the late Beryl Bainbridge's assessment of Rasputin: 'It has been written that he was one of the evilest men who ever lived. I prefer to think of him as a breath of rank air, so to speak, who blew away the cobwebs of the Imperial Palace and strode through the marble corridors in his cossack boots, ordering champagne (actually he might have preferred Madeira) by the bucket and generally being the life and soul of the party.'

For all his subsequent iconic status – and he has been celebrated and demonised almost in equal measure – there have always been those who believed in Rasputin as a Man of God. In the immediate aftermath of his death, cars and carriages pulled up at the Petrovsky Bridge, where his body had been pushed into the river; devotees were said to have come with pots, buckets and bottles to scoop up what they considered to be holy water. Later, they fought over pieces of his coffin.

Such was the fury of these 'believers' that the day after the killing Yussoupov was obliged to retreat to the Anglo-Russian hospital, apparently to have a fish bone removed. Four days later, soldiers were brought in to protect him and Grand Duke Dmitri. Munia claimed to have heard at least 20 supporters swearing vengeance.

The murder proved controversial even among Rasputin's opponents. The secret police called the conspirators 'swallows of the terror'. For all her disapproval of Rasputin, the Tsar's sister, Grand Duchess Olga, was horrified: 'There was nothing heroic about Rasputin's murder. It was... premeditated most vilely. Just think of the two names most closely associated with it even to this day – a Grand Duke, one of the grandsons of the Tsar-Liberator, and then a scion of one of our great houses whose wife was a Grand Duke's daughter. That proved how far we had fallen.' She added that the murderers had done the 'greatest disservice to one they'd sworn to serve – the Tsar'.

Grand Duke Alexander, Sandro, the man believed to have himself once plotted murder, said: 'Rasputin alive was just a man known to everybody as a drunken peasant... Rasputin dead stood a chance of becoming a slaughtered prophet.' The French Ambassador, Paleologue, who had been so critical of Rasputin, agreed: 'To the *muzhiks*, Rasputin has become a martyr. He was a man of the people, he let the Tsar hear the voice of the people; he defended the people against the Court folk, the *pridvorny*. So the *pridvorny* killed him.'

It is not unusual for followers of religious martyrs to seek out relics. In Rasputin's case, the seekers seem to have been particularly preoccupied by his penis. Maria had insisted that her father's member, when erect, stretched to a full 13 inches. This measurement probably came from the maid, Dounia, who, as his lover, might have been expected to know. But in 1914, after Rasputin was stabbed, a doctor reported that his penis was shrivelled, like that of an old man. This doctor explained that alcohol and syphilis reduced genitals and he wondered if Rasputin, then aged 45, was even potent.

Maria made much of her belief that Rasputin's murderers had cut off his penis. She described the moment with relish: 'With the skill of a surgeon these elegant members of the nobility castrated [sic] Grigory Rasputin and flung his severed penis across the room.' She was probably influenced by the 'little lady', Akilina Laptinskaya, who washed the corpse and put it in a white linen shroud. Laptinskaya was adamant that Rasputin had been mutilated.

But the pathologist Professor Dmitri Kosorotov, who conducted the four-hour autopsy, wrote in his report that the penis, though damaged, was still there: 'His genitals seem to have been crushed by the action of a similar object.' The similar object was probably Maklakov's cudgel. The soldiers who dug up Rasputin's body, after the Tsar's abdication, also saw the penis and measured it up against a brick. There is no mention in either account of the three penile warts that were said to have so improved his performance.

Several claimant penises were to appear. One became the central feature of an erotica exhibition, in 2009, at a museum in St Petersburg. The curator reported that Rasputin's penis outshone Napoleon's, which he dismissed as 'a small pod'. In 1968, Maria Rasputin's co-author, Patte Barham, visited a woman in Paris who claimed to have been given Rasputin's penis by one of Yussoupov's servants. Prayer circles were held around this penis, which lay on a velvet cloth, in an overly generous box, 18 inches long and six inches wide. She said the penis itself resembled a 'blackened over-ripe banana'.

The continued veneration of Rasputin was such that, in 1980, the lavish house at Pokrovskoye was levelled: tourists, particularly the French, were creating a nuisance by taking endless photographs. But in 1991, after the fall of the Soviet Union, a museum was opened, in a similar house, containing artefacts, documents and photographs of the village's Man of God. Visitors were invited to enhance their 'masculine powers' by sitting on Rasputin's clumpy, wooden chair.

Icons have recently begun to appear with Rasputin cradling the Tsarevich. There have even been calls within the Russian Orthodox Church for Rasputin to be canonised. Church leaders took the calls seriously enough to hold a meeting opposing the move, attended by 100 clerics in Moscow. But the Tsarina would obviously have approved; defending 'our Friend', she wrote: 'Saints are always calumniated.'

When the Imperial family's assassins stripped their victims, they found amulets around the necks of the Tsarina and the four young Grand Duchesses containing miniature portraits of Rasputin. After Rasputin's death, the Tsarina had dreamt that Brother Grigory was looking down from heaven, blessing Russia: 'He died for us,' she insisted. On December 21 1916, she wrote him a farewell letter: 'My Dear Martyr, Give me thy blessing that it may follow me always on the sad and dreary path I have yet to follow here below. And remember us from on high with your holy prayers, Alexandra.'

The letter was buried with him, along with a small bouquet of flowers. It was placed on his chest alongside the icon the Tsarina had sent him on that snowy afternoon of his final day on earth.

Bibliography

Botkin, Gleb: *The Real Romanovs* (New York, London, Edinburgh, Fleming H. Revell Company, 1931)

Cook, Andrew: *To Kill Rasputin* (Stroud, Gloucestershire, Tempus Publishing Limited, 2005)

Cullen, Richard: *Rasputin: Britain's Secret Service and the Torture and Murder of Russia's Mad Monk* (London, Dialogue, 2010)

de Jonge, Alex: *The Life and Times of Grigorii Rasputin* (London, Collins 1982)

Ferro, Marc: *Nicholas II: Last of the Tsars* (London, Viking, 1991)

Fuhrmann, Joseph T.: *Rasputin: The Untold Story* (New York, John Wiley & Sons, 2012)

Fülöp-Miller, René: *Rasputin the Holy Devil* (London & New York, GP Putnam's Sons, 1928)

Gilliard, Pierre: *Thirteen Years at the Russian Court* (Salem, New Hampshire, Ayer Company Publishers, Inc, 1994)

Hamilton, Gerald: *Blood Royal* (London, Anthony Gibbs & Phillips, Isle of Man, Times Press, 1964)

Hamilton, Gerald: *The Way It Was With Me* (London, Leslie Frewin Publishers, 1969)

King, Greg: *The Murder of Rasputin* (London, Century, 1996)

King, Greg: *The Last Empress* (London, Aurum Press, 1995)

King, Greg, and Wilson, Penny: *The Fate of the Romanovs* (Hoboken, New Jersey, John Wiley & Sons, 2003)

Massie, Robert K.: *Nicholas and Alexandra* (London, Victor Gollancz Ltd, 1968)

Milton, Giles: *Russian Roulette* (London, Sceptre, Hodder & Stoughton, 2013)

Minney, R.J.: *Rasputin* (London, The History Book Club, 1972)

Mossolov, A.A.: *At The Court Of The Last Tsar* (London, Methuen, 1935)

Moynahan, Brian: *Rasputin: The Saint Who Sinned* (London, Aurum Press, 1998)

Oakley, Jane: *Rasputin: Rascal Master* (New York, St Martin's Press, 1989)

Omessa, Charles: *Rasputin and the Russian Court* (London, George Newnes, 1918)

Pipes, Richard: *The Russian Revolution 1899–1919*, (London, Collins Harvill, 1990)

Purichkevitch, Vladimir: *Comment J'ai Tué Raspoutine* (Paris, J. Povolozky & Cie., 1924)

Radzinsky, Edward: *Rasputin: The Last Word* (London, Weidenfeld & Nicolson, 2000)

State Hermitage Museum: *Nicholas & Alexandra* (London, Booth-Clibborn Editions, 1998)

Rasputin, Maria, and Barham, Patte: *Rasputin: The Man Behind the Myth* (London, W.H. Allen, 1977)

Rasputin, Maria: *My Father* (London, Toronto, Melbourne and Sydney, Cassell and Company Ltd, 1934)

Shelayev, Yuri, Shelayeva, Elizabeth, and Semenov, Nicholas: *Nicholas Romanov: Life and Death* (St Petersburg, Liki Rossii, 2004)

Shukman, Harold: *Rasputin* (Stroud, Gloucestershire, Sutton Publishing, 1997)

Steinberg, Mark D., and Khrustalev, Vladimir M.: *The Fall Of The Romanovs* (New Haven, Connecticut and London, Yale University Press, 1995)

Symonds, John: *Conversations with Gerald* (London, Duckworth, 1974)

Tsarina Alexandra: *Last Diary of Tsarina Alexandra*

Feodorovna, 1918 (New Haven, Connecticut, Yale University Press, 1997)

Van Der Kiste, John, and Hall, Coryne: *Once a Grand Duchess, Xenia, Sister of Nicholas II* (Stroud, Gloucestershire, Sutton Publishing, 2004)

Wilson, Colin: *Rasputin and the Fall of the Romanovs* (London, Arthur Barker Ltd, 1964)

Yussoupov, Felix: *Lost Splendour* (London, Jonathan Cape, 1935)

Yussoupov, Felix: *En Exil* (Paris, Librairie Plon, 1954)

Yussoupov, Prince: *Rasputin: His Malignant Influence And His Assassination*, London, Jonathan Cape, 1927)

Other Sources:
Unpublished memoir of Prince Dmitri Romanov, property of Penny Galitzine; unpublished diaries of the British chaplain in St Petersburg, the Reverend Lombard, and letters from his grandson, John R.L. Carter. Interview with Kyril Zinovieff in Chiswick in October 2007.

Thanks to Richard Davies of the Leeds Russian Archive for sending me the Reverend Lombard's diary; Kyril Zinovieff for his generosity with his time and reminiscences; John R.L. Carter for his letters about his grandfather; Penny Galitzine for letting me use her grandfather, Prince Dmitri's, diary; Pamela Pehkonen for lending me books from her personal library; Nicholas Underhill for help with early drafts; Hugh Browton for sorting out computer glitches; Aurea Carpenter for skilled and cheerful editing; finally, my family, Craig, Tallulah and Silas, for putting up with me as I joined, briefly, the 'Rasputinki'.